ACKNOWLEDGMENT

This magazine has been published by Wharncliffe History Magazines in association with Pen and Sword Military Books Limited, with the purpose of creating an awareness and an interest in the subject of military history.

For over twenty years Pen and Sword has published numerous military, naval and aviation books covering various conflicts throughout history. A vast amount of military titles have been published over the past few years, covering the personal accounts of soldiers who have taken part in many conflicts, stretching from the First World War through to the Falklands War. The books featured in this magazine are only a few titles taken from a large selection of subjects covering special forces units.

These publications would not have been possible if it had not been for the skill and dedication of the authors, who have painstakingly researched and written about these conflicts in order to bring them to light.

Only extracts have been taken from these titles to produce this magazine and much more information can be gleaned by reading the books mentioned at the end of each chapter. Pen and Sword have added more colour illustrations and images to the text in order to add more for the reader, making this a very special publication.

Pen and Sword Military Books would like to thank; John Lewes, Carol Mather, Lorna Almonds Windmill, Harold Challenor, Alfred Draper, Francis MacKay, Jon Cooksey, John Simpson, Mark Adkin, Robert Jackson, William Seymour and Ian Gardiner, whose works have appeared in this magazine SAS – THE HISTORY OF THE SPECIAL AIR SERVICE REGIMENT.

Wharncliffe
HISTORY MAGAZINES

In association with;

Pen & Sword Military Books.

First published in Great Britain in 2009 by
Wharncliffe History Magazines
47 Church Street
Barnsley
South Yorkshire
S70 2AS

Copyright © Wharncliffe Publishing, 2009

Edited by Roni Wilkinson

Design, layout, maps & photograph colouring:
Jon Wilkinson

ISBN: 978 184884 156 7

A CIP catalogue record for this book is
available from the British Library.

Printed and bound in the United Kingdom

For a complete list of Pen & Sword titles please
contact
PEN & SWORD BOOKS LIMITED
47 Church Street, Barnsley, South Yorkshire,
S70 2AS, England
E-mail: enquiries@pen-and-sword.co.uk
Website: www.pen-and-sword.co.uk

CONTENTS

INTRODUCTION

The SAS burst onto the stage of public awareness in highly dramatic style. Thirty years ago families returning home after a day's outing on Bank Holiday Monday, 5 May 1980, were treated to a ringside seat, viewing on their television screens blow by blow actions of a mysterious, masked, black-clad military unit engaged in rescuing hostages and in ruthlessly executing their terrorist captives with lethal and accurate gunfire.

The assault on the Iranian Embassy, Prince's Gate, London began exactly twenty-three minutes after a murdered hostage was pushed through the Embassy's front door. For many it was the merciless, cold-blooded efficiency of the rescuers that stunned the senses – these men were Government agents 'licensed to kill'! This was in a society where the police force prided itself on carrying out its duties unarmed. Obviously, the mystery unit belonged to the British Army and its soldiers seemed capable of carrying out dangerous and difficult operations. Their success could only be attributed to a high degree of specialised training, which was unavailable to the conventional infantryman. Within hours, 'SAS' was on the lips of the nation and indeed, virtually the whole world carried the story and was talking about this British special services unit – the Special Air Service.

Public fascination was further fuelled by the anonymity – as a matter of policy – insisted upon by the soldiers, and conveyed through their spokesman. Ever since then, the public could not hear or read enough of the doings of the SAS. Other cold-blooded dispatching of dangerous activists followed. But now the press and public, fully alerted, were attributing every incident to the mysterious SAS. But with the British Government operating a policy of cautionary or non-disclosure concerning the SAS much had to remain speculation.

Conventional warfare, such as the Falklands War, revealed how the SAS was employed along with regular formations; for example, the raid on Pebble Island which resulted in the destruction of Argentinian aircraft. This was all much in the style of the Royal Marine Commandos.

However, there is much more to the SAS, and hostage situations have served to illustrate this. For example, in September 2000 there was the rescue of six captured Royal Irish Rangers in Sierra Leone. Then there is the averting of incidents by initiating action against perceived threats. This is seen in the summary execution on the street of three IRA suspects in Gibraltar, March 1988 (or did the perpetrators belong to another government agency?).

Where did this elite force come from? How did such a lethal unit find its place on the British Army list? What kind of men volunteer for such a highly motivated and efficient killing machine?

It all began with raids against Rommel's Afrika Korps and the Italians in the Western Desert in 1941. The outfit was the brain-child of David Stirling and Jock Lewes and operated in conjunction with the Long Range Desert Group. Extracts from the book by John Lewes relates how this all came about and descriptions of the very first desert raids. Jock Lewes was killed in December 1941 and David Stirling was captured in January 1943. It was left to others to carry on.

Carol Mather took part in those early raids and his experiences help us to see how the potential of the SAS, as an irregular fighting unit, was beginning to develop. Unlike the LRDG, it was never intended that the SAS confine its operations to just one particular type of warfare, and the Special Boat Service was born. Raids on the German occupied islands in the Mediterranean, although pin pricks, served to keep the enemy on its toes. The story of George, 2nd Earl Jellicoe, covers some 'hits' on the island of Crete, extracts of which are included here.

What were these men like who volunteered for incredibly dangerous operations behind enemy lines? The amazing story of Tanky Challenor gives us a glimpse into the make-up of the rank and file and how their experiences could leave them seriously affected (post-traumatic stress). Tanky's fighting experiences are included here; for the rest of his story – post war – his book *Tanky Challenor – SAS and the Met* should be consulted.

Dropped by parachute into occupied France, the SAS operatives had their parts to play in covert operations prior to D-Day. Following which they ranged deep behind enemy lines in their preferred transport – the Jeep. Here also is the story of the legendary Roy Farran.

At the end of the war, amazingly, the Special Air Service was disbanded, only to be revived in an emergency to deal with the many outbreaks of terrorism as post-war 'freedom fighters' struggled to assert their dominance. Specifically, the Communist threat in Malaya.

Wherever people live under the ever-present threat of terrorist indiscriminate actions against the populace, the ordinary person-in-the-street can find some comfort in knowing that there exists an extension of the police force, that is trained, equipped and prepared to rescue them and their loved ones should the need arise.

PEN & SWORD MILITARY BOOKS

 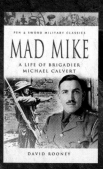 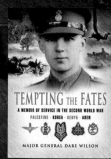  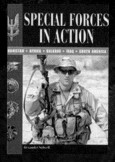 

SECRET FORCES OF WORLD WAR II

One of the lasting legacies of World War II was the proliferation of what today are known as Special Forces. At the time many soldiers, often of high rank regarded these units as nothing short of ill-disciplined cowboys or worse! However desperate times called for desperate measures and there were those in high places who were prepared to take risks. As specially recruited units such as the LRDG, SAS and SBS earned their spurs and scored significant victories, at high cost both to the enemy and themselves, so faith in the concept grew.

ISBN: 184415114X • Pbk • **£12.99**

MAD MIKE
A LIFE OF BRIGADIER MICHAEL CALVERT

This penetrating biography tells the story of Calvert's life including his exploits in Norway and the early Commandos. It also uncovers new evidence revealing that his court martial was unjust.

ISBN: 9781844155071 • Pbk • **£9.99**

TEMPTING THE FATES
A MEMOIR OF SERVICE IN THE SECOND WORLD WAR, PALESTINE, KOREA, KENYA, ADEN

General Dare Wilson saw action in France 1940 (Dunkirk), Italy and North West Europe (where he won his MC) with the Northumberland Fusiliers and later the Recce Regiment. He then served in Palestine and Korea which he rates as the most vicious war he fought in. He was picked to command 22 SAS and was responsible for basing them at Hereford. His account of the world record-breaking free fall jump free falling from 34,000 feet makes thrilling reading. He went on to fight the Mau Mau in Kenya and was in the last party to leave Aden when we withdrew in 1968. Dare then learnt to fly helicopters and commanded the fledgling Army/Air Corps. We believe that this is one of the most enthralling of the many superb memoirs we have published. Certainly it is the widest in its scope and makes for gripping reading.

ISBN: 9781844154357 • Hbk • **£19.99**

ENCYCLOPEDIA OF ELITE FORCES IN THE SECOND WORLD WAR

The Second World War saw the formation and employment of a large number of specialist units in all the many theatres. The most celebrated Special Forces were the units such as the SAS, Long Range Desert Group and the American OSS but this book looks at the much wider spectrum. It embraces special-to-purpose formations such as the Chindits, parachute forces of Germany and the Allies, specially formed air force units such as the Dambusters, Hans-Ulrich Rudel's Tank-Busting Stuka Squadrons, the US Flying Tigers and the Doolittle Raiders and Memphis Belle Bomber team. At sea the activities of the midget submarine crews, torpedo craft operators and the mighty German battleships are examined. All this and much more besides make *Elite Forces of the Second World War* a thrilling, highly informative and most attractive book.

ISBN: 9781844155774 • Hbk • **£19.99**

SPECIAL FORCES IN ACTION

Since the end of the Cold War there have been numerous conflicts and in all of these Special Forces have played a key role. This book examines their activities and operations in numerous theatres from Afghanistan and, Iraq today to the Balkans and Gulf War. Lesser known small wars such as Sierra Leone (and the spectacular rescue of British soldiers by the SAS) and Somalia are also well covered. We learn of long running drug busting operations in Colombia and of current operations pursuing war criminals in the Balkans. In addition there is an introductory chapter tracing the development of SF from their inception in the Second World War with brief descriptions of early operations.

ISBN: 9781844155583 • Hbk • **£19.99**

SPECIAL OPERATIONS IN IRAQ

This sensational book reveals the true and compelling story of the Special Force units of the Coalition, such as the SAS, SBS and Delta Force who worked in the shadows, often unseen, unheard and unsung. It describes their missions behind the lines from the early days, well before hostilities opened formally. It was an open secret that groups were deployed probably operating in the western desert against Saddam's forces and the Scud missile threat. What was actually going on is revealed here and until now their roles and actions have not been described in any detail.

ISBN: 1844153274 • Pbk • **£12.99**

'Prove it! The trouble with you people you've all got a bloody yellow streak a yard wide down your backs! You just can't take it...unless you can prove otherwise.'

JOCK LEWES TO SEASONED AND TRIED EX-COMMANDO VOLUNTEERS FOR THE NEW ÉLITE UNIT

THE STRUGGLE TO EXIST

Credit for the formation in 1941 of the Special Air Service, today the World's most respected special force, has traditionally been given to David Stirling. This, as those 'in the know' acknowledge, is only part of the truth. Jock Lewes, a young Welsh Guards officer, was at least equally responsible. Without his and David Stirling's partnership there would have been no SAS. Stirling was later to chivalrously admit: 'Jock Lewes could far more genuinely claim to be founder of the Special Air Service than I'.

By John Lewes

Extracted from *Jock Lewes, Co-founder of the SAS* and reproduced by permission of Pen & Sword Books Ltd.

David Stirling's genius lay in his recognition of Jock Lewes' ideas and his determination to exploit them at all costs. Stirling forced his way into the heart of British Middle East Headquarters (MEHQ) to present the concept of the Special Air Service on a unit basis to General Ritchie. It was the only way a junior officer in his position might be listened to. The prospect of a court-martial was an extra incentive in Stirling's first of many bold acts to join with Lewes, in order to fashion a group of volunteer parachutists into the SAS Regiment. Stirling obtained permission from MEHQ to go ahead with what became known as 'Stirling's Rest Camp'. Jock Lewes agreed to join in the new venture and bring all his experience and ideas with him.

He immediately recruited NCOs from Tobruk who were of outstanding quality and would form the vital backbone of the unit. In later years David Stirling explained why he had sought to win over Jock Lewes to the concept of a parachute raiding formation:

'I think he was the greatest training officer of the last war. The men had a huge respect for him. You can see how important he was for me, how I had to persuade him to join me.'

Jock took a scholarly approach to the training and examined the new recruits after only a week's work. Reg Seekings, later Stirling's bodyguard and a highly decorated NCO, remembered how they were each given an exercise book and regularly tested and marked on everything they learned.

Jock Lewes, a co-founder of the SAS.

David Stirling.

Throughout Jock's brief experience of soldiering, he had been constantly mindful of the need to gain the respect of his own men before attempting to seek laurels from his superiors, and this want weighed heavily upon him as he began the establishment of a fully operational SAS unit.

In the first week of September 1941, when Jock imposed a regime that appeared to consist of more mindless routines of digging the Libyan Desert to soften up the ground for the detachment's tent posts, he nearly witnessed a mutiny that might have resulted in his dismemberment by a lynch mob of hitherto leaderless soldiers.

Sergeant Major Yates was in charge of a very basic SAS camp that caused tensions when Seekings and Jock first arrived at its location in Kabrit. Yates had little in the way of food except bully beef, biscuits, herrings and porridge, let alone equipment. Reg Seekings recalled, *'The food was terrible and there was no organization.'* The Commandos who joined the SAS had opted for special service but were in a sense on probation. Once failed, they were informed that SAS servicemen would be permanently returned to their original unit which was anathema to most soldiers who would then suffer the indignity of being branded unsatisfactory for the fledgling SAS.

Jock kept the men occupied in training with great purpose; it was tailored to suit the needs of anyone who could stay the course. Old factories were blown up, there was plenty of PT in the mornings, night schemes with

Kabrit Camp was the first base for the newly-created raiding force, the Special Air Service.

method of escape from a target area that would often be attacked in darkness. By Saturday, 28 September the recruits were engaged in a thirty-mile night scheme and spent Sunday recovering; the first intensive training must have been backbreaking work. They would eventually build up to a ninety-five mile march over three days and four nights in the possible event of their needing that mobility. Little was left to chance as it had been for some of these men in the Commandos.

The men knew little of why Stirling was frequently absent in Cairo, where he steadily developed the contacts necessary to win the support of the middle managers at MEHQ, who were not 'with him or Lewes' and therefore 'against them'. Peter Stirling, David's brother, was attached to the British Embassy in Cairo and his flat was a useful base from which to gather the latest information before a host of double agents that appeared to infest Cairo got there first. In late 1941 Stirling managed to have dinner several times with the Countess of Ranfurly, who was secretary to both Generals Wilson and Alexander during the war. The Countess was one of the few English women in the Middle East who obtained access to sensitive information that could be invaluable when advising young ambitious officers. She was a model of discretion, but it is possible that she may have been able to help Stirling with the necessary contacts in order to help launch the conflict in the Middle East from the First World War into the Second.

What the men at training at Kabrit needed most was a strict officer, who was going to enable them to look on their preparation as the best way to endure combat with superior forces behind the German and Italian lines.

Jock's emotional resilience in all his planning for the unit would achieve his and Stirling's objectives, rather than being the heart and soul of the party in the canteen with the rest of the men after training was over.

There were three other officers to assist Jock. Lieutenant Fraser helped out with map-reading, Lieutenant Eion MacGonigal was a first-class weapons instructor and Lieutenant Blair Mayne was PT instructor and also responsible for any punishments that needed meting out – which in effect meant doing several rounds in the ring with him. It may have been less daunting for the likes of highly professional soldiers such as Seekings and Riley, who had also boxed each other at Wisbech before the war, but Paddy Mayne was seventeen stone and usually 'a few quiet words' from him was enough to persuade any recalcitrant soldier that discretion was the better part of valour where training was concerned.

Ernie Bond, David Stirling's Platoon Sergeant, recalled that Jock was largely responsible for all the ideas and schemes that developed the SAS in 1941 and

navigation by the stars, and intelligence-gathering by lying out in the hills to observe enemy patrols and air observation. Reg Seekings considered Jock's instruction on medical care in the desert as the best the detachment were offered until Dr Pleydell worked with the SAS in 1942, and Pat Riley remembers that Jock even explained the importance of handling a plane on land in case any of the men required an emergency exit from an enemy aerodrome. Jock created treasure hunts to develop navigation and used Kirn's Game to sharpen wits; blindman's bluff in the tent developed sensitivity in the dark and made work a pleasure rather than humdrum routine.

He had promised that the men of the SAS Brigade would be ten times tougher than the Commandos. The men might get a beer in the early evening, but they were often back on duty for 10.00 pm for night marching in order to realize the super-awareness they were honing in Jock's games. It was the only time to train the all-important

Lieutenant Blair Mayne.

enabled the men to hit targets and escape largely undetected:

> 'Jock was the thinker, he used to think the "whys and wherefores". Everyone thought, "We'll do this, get there and do the other," but little attention was paid as to how we were going to get out. David Stirling wanted the action without the preparation and training. I wonder whether David would have ever survived without Jock. None of the other officers were of Jock's calibre to take on the roles he did and all the preparation for operations that he took on.'

Reg Seekings confirmed that 'Jock had a bit of help' from the others, but the onus of planning depended upon him and explains why his lantern burned late on into the lonely nights.

Jock expected others to do what he himself could do; where he could lead them they must follow, for he was as severe on others as he was hard on himself. He drew out plans and timetables for the training. How should they best become fit so that this sort of warfare could be rewarded with tangible results?... Wasn't there some story that in England parachute troops were jumping from moving lorries? He tried the theories out, one after another. He jumped from a truck travelling at twenty miles an hour and did a forward roll. 'All right', he cried out as he picked himself up, 'that's OK' and he put it down in the training syllabus. Then he jumped backwards from the truck travelling at the same speed, but in doing so he hurt himself. Accordingly the exercise was ruled out, for there was no object in causing more casualties than were necessary over the training itself.

He did injure himself and indirectly others in the process of parachute practice: three had suffered broken arms and others suffered more breaks by the first week in October 1941. Jock's baptism of fire with the men

Another method of parachute training employed by the SAS. Here two recruits are seen disembarking from a moving trolley which has been propelled along rails.

was not over immediately: Pat Riley, who later became training officer, remembered that, 'Stirling was away for most of 1941,' and Jock, largely on his own, had much to prove to the men on his and Stirling's behalf. Perhaps it would have been less possible for David Stirling to be so soft-spoken, fair, firm and good-humoured without the powerful internal chemistry of the SAS, which under Jock's leadership was steadily developing and which Stirling was protecting in Cairo.

Parachute training and simulation for practice jumps had originally been made from wooden platforms set on

Recruits undergoing a dangerous parachute training exercise by rolling off the back of a moving truck.

Jock Lewes leading parachute training jumps at the Special Air Service camp at Kabrit.

trolleys and in mid-October tall towers were made. A miniature railway in an old quarry in Kabrit had been used for the trolleys. Soldiers pushed the trolley, which then gathered speed until it eventually came to a rise and a stop; a PT instructor would tell what sort of roll they wanted and when. This still did not simulate the appropriate force of landing, which was similar to jumping off a fifteen-foot wall, and therefore the detachment's designer (and much more besides), Jim Almonds, set to work on three forty-foot steel towers known as the 'Wedding Ring Assembly'. Advice from the parachute centre at Ringway, Manchester, was slow in coming, so the pioneers made do with the towers that enabled a parachutist to simulate landing in the wind; Jim noted that, *'it gave you the impression that you steered.'* The towers were attached to an iron ring around which the parachutist manoeuvred; the whole contraption was very heavy and, because the SAS lacked extra help, the towers were used and fortunately never collapsed, but they were potentially 'very dangerous'. The men ascended a small tower, put their harnesses on and jumped off with a big swing, descending slowly and finishing with a forward or backward roll.

Jock had already prepared practice jumps from 2,000 feet from the old

Valentia plane that he had borrowed in June, and used in Bagoush. The SAS had acquired, for the same purpose, a Bombay, which was considerably more suitable than the Valentia. However, its tail was set too low in relation to the fuselage to allow safe practice, and it had ripped some of the men's chutes as they left the aircraft. On 17 October disaster struck. A fault in the clip attaching the static line to the rail meant that if the line twisted from the effects of the slipstream, that kind of line could detach itself. All the parachutists prepared to jump with this equipment. Two men, to everyone's horror, jumped from the plane and thudded into the gound in front of Stirling, who with Jock, had previously made safe landings that morning. The two victims both died. The despatcher, Flight Sergeant Ted Pacey, and sometimes known as 'The Blue Orchid' was a man who was known to 'take you over'. On this occasion Pacey 'took over' the third man's attempt to leave the aircraft and saved his life. The morale of the whole unit was in jeopardy. Decisive leadership was needed in order to win back any lost confidence; parachute practice was halted for that day. In 1987 Bob Bennet remembered that:

'Lewes had us on parade, told us that... it was due to the fact that the RAF had put the fitting

An aged Vickers Valentia used by Jock for parachute training.

Bristol Bombay.

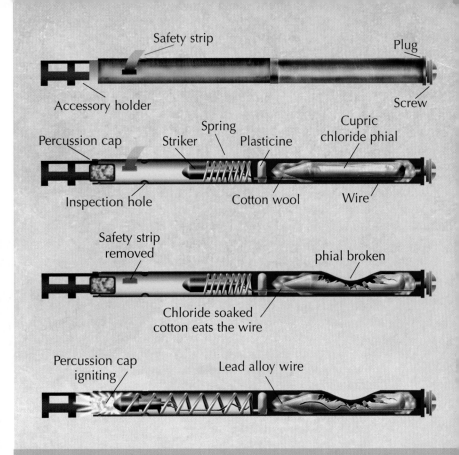

Safety strip
Plug
Accessory holder
Screw

Percussion cap
Spring
Cupric chloride phial
Striker
Plasticine

Inspection hole
Cotton wool
Wire

Safety strip removed
phial broken

Chloride soaked cotton eats the wire

Percussion cap igniting
Lead alloy wire

THE TIME PENCIL

of the Bombay in the hands of the Egyptians. Lewes said this would be put right, "the RAF would do it in future. Anyone that wants to leave is welcome to go." This is when I found out I was with a unit that meant something, because not one man backed out.'

Pat Riley, who jumped second in the next practice jump with a new clip that was substituted, recalled that on 18 October the first man to jump after stronger clips replaced the faulty ones was Jock Lewes. Stirling jumped too, but it would have been appropriate for Jock to jump first as Training Officer, and Pat Riley added, *'I know because I was right behind him.'*

Without the relevant technology, the embryonic SAS unit might have faded away, for General Ritchie's continued support of the SAS could only be based on its results. There was a dearth of manpower and the detachment could only exist and continue recruiting from other units if it could prove that ten of its men could destroy as many targets as 100 Commandos.

At that stage of the war, without a lightweight bomb, the SAS could only be useful for limited raids and intelligence gathering; however, the LRDG had already been filling the last role for over a year. Ernie Bond remembered how Jock spent several weeks experimenting with explosives in any spare time he could afford. It must have been clear to both Stirling and Lewes that a solution to the problem had to be found and quickly. The pressures came not only from MEHQ, but also from the fact that, if the men had been asked to train for action in the desert, there had better be some.

Jock procured an old wing of a plane that he placed on some large oil drums, so that he could blow a hole in the wing and ignite the fuel in the tanks inside. In early October, it would have been normal for men at Kabrit to be training away or writing letters after exercises with very little peace during either activity: small explosions from Jock's makeshift laboratory punctuated the day, ringing out like a loose cannon. It seems that the SAS Training Officer would not rest until he had made the 'impossible' possible.

Both David Stirling and Jock found great solace in inviting the Ordnance Major for a little demonstration. For Ernie Bond recalled how one day Jock, *'erupted with joy shouting, "Oil! Of course oil!" and hugged several innocent by-standers'*; the experimental aircraft wing had been blown up but also now gushed with fire. Jock had developed a practical bomb through sheer persistence. He had obtained some of the new plastic explosive that he then rolled successfully into a mixture of old engine oil and thermite from an incendiary bomb. A time pencil activated the explosion. It consisted of acid that would eat away through a wire connected to the

plunger of a No. 27 detonator. Different strengths of acid gave time delays of between ten minutes and hours if need be. The plastic bomb, which was an unstable mixture, could be packed into the hollow tubing of an aircraft seat, so that the explosion might take place days after a raid. Jimmy Storie suggested this was another way *'to put the fear of God into the enemy'*. The oil made it that much more malleable, so that the new bombs could also be shaped into tennis-ball-sized explosives, if required, and set up in seconds. A crowd of sceptical sappers and RAF officers saw small pliable lumps of explosive being quickly assembled and effectively used on an aircraft wing; a large number of bombs could be carried by one man. The Ordnance Major accepted that the latest weapon in his armoury should be called the 'Lewes Bomb'. With the Lewes Bombs (or 'sticky' bombs) Jock had provided the first SAS unit with the 'teeth' it so badly needed.

REHEARSAL

A dress rehearsal of an actual desert raid was now a

The Lewes 'sticky' Bomb.

realistic ambition for the SAS unit. Much of the timing of Jock's training programme and invention of his bomb was in rhythm with the development of his men who were ready for the promised action. Within weeks of the Lewes Bomb's invention, another sceptic provided the fillip for more leadership from Lewes and Stirling and yet more daring from the men.

A certain Group Captain of the RAF was sent by Ritchie to evaluate Jock's training methods and chances of successfully raiding an airfield. The RAF Officer, whose name has been lost, apparently decided that it was an impertinence of David Stirling to suggest that raiding an

General Auchinleck.

airfield was quite within the gift of the SAS. The Group Captain was certainly piqued when the Scotsman considered the real challenge lay in being accurately dropped on target by the RAF. Stirling, a clever talker and salesman who could talk anyone into anything, baited the RAF Officer to offer his own airfield as a target exercise for the SAS, as they had been recently inspired by their confidence to place charges on their objectives. Stirling, who always considered money should be used rather than saved, also lured the Group Captain into laying £10 that the parachutists could not get onto his airfield at Heliopolis at any time they wished in order to position stickers – rather than 'sticky' bombs – to prove that the aerodrome could be successfully attacked.

The mock raid on the RAF airfield at Heliopolis near Cairo was a turning point in SAS morale and development. The 'sticky' labels representing the recently invented Lewes Bomb were carried by five officers and their men inside a sixty-pound pack, each containing supplies that included only four bottles of water and three pounds of dates for personal consumption during the three hot days and four freezing nights out in the desert. In groups of ten men Lieutenants Lewes, Bonnington, Fraser, MacGonigal and Mayne set out from Kabrit at night, camouflaging themselves in rocky escarpments in the day with the assistance of shadow and pieces of hessian sacking. Jimmie Storie, who was in Jock's party, remembers that the group managed to overcome the risks of hallucination and deprivation in the cloudless skies that burned the parachutists in the day and froze them during the night.

Jock's men entered Heliopolis airfield in a novel fashion. Apparently Jock had decided that through the airfield's soft underbelly the men would have less wire cutting to do: once inside the RAF kitchen, they would 'persuade' the staff to show them the least conspicuous route in and out. It was a great success as were all the other sticks of parachutists: none of them had seen each

> 'Never run; once you start running you stop thinking.'
>
> JOCK LEWES

other, but all the aircraft were labelled, some with several stickers from different groups; the ears of senior officers at MEHQ were 'blistered' by the SAS operation, because none of the daily spotter planes had observed the raiders. This made more gestures of despair and doubting from administrators at MEHQ indefensible.

The fledgling SAS unit was ready for its first operational task, and Operation *Crusader* seemed to be just what the Brigade could assist with. Auchinleck's plan for this offensive was to push Rommel out of Cyrenaica in the largest armoured operation undertaken by the British at that time. Auchinleck was under pressure from Churchill to begin the next phase of the desert war which was a renewed effort to drive back the Italians and Germans. The offensive would stand a greater chance of success if parachutists destroyed enemy planes before Operation *Crusader*, and if the raid failed MEHQ had only lost a handful of men with no great drain on their resources. The recently formed Eighth Army were to obtain airfields, partly to protect convoys to Malta after relieving the garrison of Tobruk. The SAS mission was to begin on the night of 17 November 1941 and the parachutists' role was potentially vital in reducing enemy air attacks during the following day. Auchinleck paid a visit to Kabrit days before the SAS were dropped near the enemy's airfields in the area of Gazala and Tmimi, in recognition of the parachutists' achievements, and no doubt also meant as a great morale booster before their first dangerous mission.

Then came the dreaded news, Stirling and Lewes were told that, due to the poor conditions, whether the SAS mission went ahead or not was up to them, but the General Staff had suggested it would be suicide to continue with the task. The men were informed of the dangers, but it seems that all ranks agreed that, in order to maintain their credibility as a new unit, to resign from the opportunity to strike the enemy would possibly jeopardize their military stock with MEHQ. Whatever decision was made it would involve great risks as far as Stirling and Lewes were concerned. Yet as the leading officers they bore much responsibility for supporting Operation *Crusader* against the advice in all the meteorological reports.

Navigating the aircraft into the dropping zone would be difficult from the outset. The pilots were flying the first troops in converted bombers whose centre of gravity moved eleven feet every time a parachutist moved down the fuselage to the rear gun turret, which had been transformed into a lavatory. Even if the force was dropped they might lose the cover of darkness regrouping their scattered and injured men. Stirling and

Lewes had little choice but to take the only chance that critical rivals might give them from the administrative centre at MEHQ. The men wanted to continue despite the obvious risks, and their officers were not keen to cancel their first SAS raid, even though there was great chance of failure. There had been too many pressures from headquarters that suggested that any excuse could be used to disband the new force: the enemies of the 'new learning' drove the SAS Brigade between Scylla and Charybdis.

Five detachments of men were guided by the same officers that succeeded in the Heliopolis raid except that this time Stirling led his own group and Lieutenant Fraser joined Jock. Sergeant 'Gentleman' Jim Almonds kept watch at camp, because he expected immediate recall to England as both his son, and wife, May, were suffering ill health. Jock would have missed the presence of Jim in his group because the two had worked well together in Tobruk and the latter was an excellent navigator. Like Jock, Jim was convinced of the promise that his unit displayed, and on the day of the operation wrote,

The two founders of the Special Air Service, David Stirling (left) and Jock Lewes plotting something unpleasant for Rommel and his Afrika Korps.

> *'Reality beats fiction for sheer, cold, calculating courage. More will be heard of the SAS should this raid go as planned.'*

Jock contented himself with the company of Sergeant Pat Riley, later the SAS RSM, also battle-worn from Tobruk and another staunch ally. Pat Riley was both very tough and physically strong, and it seems that the SAS was the perfect outlet for his considerable energy and flair in a brawl. Reg Seekings recalled that earlier that year, in scrapes with the military police, Pat had managed to flatten the Provost Marshal in Cairo. However, at the inception of the SAS unit, aggression was reserved for the enemy.

FAILURE

Jock's Bristol Bombay took off in winds of about thirty-five mph at about 7.30 pm on 16 November 1941 from 216 Squadron's forward base at Bagoush. He and all the officers in their respective Bombays checked each man's kit which included a small spade that every parachutist had recently been issued with. It could be used to bury the parachute or even dig a foxhole if necessary. The short implement was fitted inside the parachutist's waist belt and rested parallel with the soldier's spine. Before leaving the aerodrome. Jock had warned his men to compensate as best they could for what was now becoming atrocious weather. In his memoir, *One of the*

'The force of hitting the ground would have been far greater than the impact of jumping off a five foot wall. Most men suffered a severe jolt throughout the body.'

'Originals' Johnny Cooper gives a detailed account of Jock's first officially backed mission. Cooper, then the youngest in Jock's party, recalled how his leader alerted them to the wind speed, which he would give the men minutes before jumping, and the way he prepared them for the landing itself:

> *'Now remember this lads, set the back bearing on your compasses and you will have the best chance of locating the man who has jumped before you.'*

The pilot of the Bristol Bombay was aiming to clear the coastal strip with its Italian ground defences, which were always ready to gun the high-flying RAF bombers that targeted Axis supply lines and the port of Benghazi. Although Jock's plane flew low to avoid the enemy anti-aircraft attacks, they were still pinpointed by searchlights. With magnificent flying, the RAF pilot avoided most of the flak. The green light came on not long after the aircraft was hit, but the shell did no serious damage and by then the coast was clear. Jock warned the men that the plane's course was off target, because of the recent attacks combined with the wind speed that was by then force nine. The navigator gave the parachutists the wind direction and then the whole stick quickly jumped.

The force of hitting the ground would have been far greater than the impact of jumping off a five foot wall. Most men suffered a severe jolt throughout the body. After that, most were at first unable to gather themselves and their parachutes up, because the wind was dragging

THOMPSON SUB-MACHINE GUN

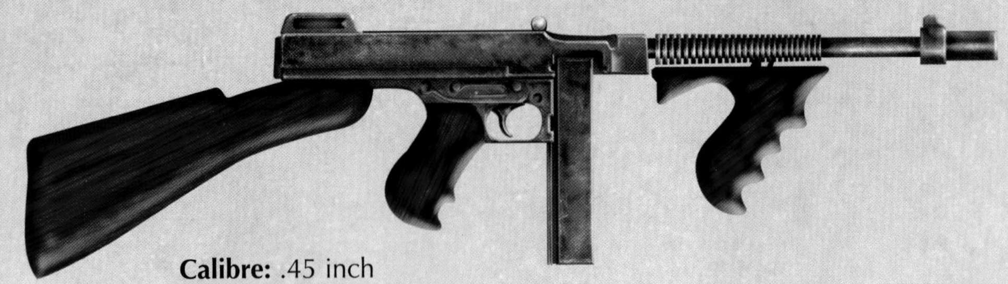

Calibre: .45 inch	
Muzzle velocity: 918 ft/s	
Operation type: Selective fire, fully and semi-automatic	
Weight: 10 lbs	
Magazine: 20 round box or a 50 and 100 round drum magazine. A 30 round box magazine was introduced in 1942	

ILLUSTRATION BY: JON WILKINSON

them at thirty miles an hour. Staggering neat landings was an impossibility, but every parachutist who left that plane had been reminded of their responsibility in locating the man who had just parachuted before them. Reg Seekings, in Lieutenant Mayne's group, remembered that most of his exposed skin was scraped off by being dragged by a still inflated parachute over small rocks and gravel. His parachute straps had snagged around the end of his spade.

Few of the men were fully aware of why some of them had been dragged well after they had pressed the quick release box into which the straps of their harness were clamped. In such conditions, some had failed to turn to unlock the release button, others had actually followed the correct procedure but immediately encountered a problem that they may have been oblivious to. The small spades that were worn behind them had never been used in a training jump and, although some of the parachutists did release their parachute, the straps of the harness caught around the spade and its handle. Therefore, men continued to be dragged across the stony floor of the desert, and this proved fatal in many cases. Reg Seekings survived this particular ordeal, and one of many important lessons was learnt.

Jock led the only party of men where every parachutist was located. Learning by experience was the SAS' hard school. Johnny Cooper gratefully acknowledged his fortune in being one of the men who had not been lost with the forty who had been mostly killed or captured:

'I was lucky, I was with Jock. We all got together, the only complete stick of the twenty-two that came back. Johnny Cooper walked along the compass bearing provided by the navigator and met one of the group. Sergeant Jimmie Storie found his friend, Jock Cheyne, also in Jock Lewes' stick; Jock Cheyne was tall

'After a night of torrential rain their compasses were redundant and Jock decided that his group had been dispatched far off their dropping zone.'

and the ordeal had left him with injuries that meant he had a better chance of survival as an Italian or German prisoner. Jimmie wanted to carry him, but it was impossible, and so Jock Cheyne huddled into the blankets that were brought him, and later it was thought that he must have died there.'

The original intention of moving forward to the escarpment, in order to attack the enemy airfield the following night, was out of the question. Even though Jock's men had recovered all their food, water, Thompson machine guns and equipment, bar two hard-cardboard containers, there was nothing for them to blow up. The only course left open to them was to try and locate their rendezvous point with the LRDG at Rotunda Segnale. After a night of torrential rain their compasses were redundant and Jock decided that his group had been dispatched far off their dropping zone. All the Lewes Bombs were destroyed with a timed explosion, but they may well have been rendered useless, because not long afterwards the soldiers ceased to be short of water: the whole desert was swimming in several inches of it. The worst hurricane and rainstorm that had been recorded in thirty years. Electrical storms had affected their compass navigation. They knew they had travelled in a circuitous route, because, by the time the Lewes Bombs went off, the men could hear the explosion close by. Fortunately it became warmer and the visibility increased, which helped because the terrain around them remained featureless for miles.

In the white molten heat of the day they marched in a south-westerly direction towards what they hoped would be the Trig al Abd, a so-called road, running thirty miles south of the coast between the Cyrenaican and Egyptian borders. Fortified by chocolate, emergency rations, biscuits and, on this occasion, plenty of water, the men were led by 'the young eyes' of Johnny Cooper, who noticed a signpost on the horizon. Jock quickly asked, 'But will it be pointing in the right direction and will it have anything written on it?' Jock turned west in the direction of Benghazi, Sergeant Yates in Stirling's group also reached the Trig al Abd, but marched in the opposite direction towards Sollum and eventually into an enemy patrol. Jock met Stirling who was accompanied by Sergeant Tait, and with most of Lieutenant Mayne's stick they counted the dead. The SAS had lost forty of the sixty-two men, and Jim Almonds reported that it 'must have been hell' for the survivors 'are a tight-lipped lot'. The loss of so many of the unit was a tragedy few could have predicted, and it seemed that its future was in jeopardy. Lewes and Stirling were now in danger of having their plans for the SAS shelved at a most vulnerable point of its development.

WINNING COMBINATION – CRY HAVOC!

Lewes' organization of the SAS enabled the force to win an opportunity to stage another raid a month later. Most of the parachutists who survived the treacherous conditions of this raid foiled the sceptics at MEHQ by marching nearly fifty miles across the desert to their rendezvous and established that, under the most exacting circumstances. Jock's training enabled them to be mobile behind enemy lines without detection. Also with the LRDG patrol's successful recovery of the marchers, the new unit displayed a great strength in failure, which augured well for succeeding operations which could guarantee better conditions and greater success. As they were able to carry enough lightweight bombs, it seemed plausible that they could destroy airfields and return to their rendezvous points in the worst weather conditions.

First, they had to take stock, of men, equipment and the lessons that they had learned on the way. The LRDG could help the SAS further by transporting the parachutists to a new base from where they could achieve success in new raids. Lewes and Stirling needed to overcome their recent abortive raid with an effective assault on Axis airfields – before making contact with MEHQ, who otherwise might conspire to suspend or cease SAS operations.

The LRDG badge.

The Libyan Desert stretches a thousand miles southward from the Mediterranean and even further west from the Nile valley to Tunisia: west to east it is Paris to Warsaw, north to south, Leeds to Barcelona. Most of it is desert with some areas of spectacular scenery. Major Ralph Bagnold, who formed the Long Range Desert Group in 1940, could only find one small-scale map that extended beyond the western frontier of Egypt, containing mostly information gathered by Rohlfs, a Victorian explorer. Wavell appointed Bagnold to create a mobile scouting force to gather information on the Italians, whose motorized units posed a threat to the Egypt-Sudan line of communication at Wadi Haifa. Bagnold had offered Wavell 'piracy on the high desert' and this was accepted in the LRDG's role. It is probable that the formation of the SAS in September forced General Auchinleck's hand in fully extending the use of the LRDG, especially as David Lloyd Owen had offered to ferry the SAS to and from their targets.

The Long Range Desert Group had managed to create a 'sand-screen' of movement and attacks that exaggerated its strength in 1940 by appearing 600 miles apart, and it destroyed 2,500 gallons of fuel north of Kufra; at the time when Italian troops outnumbered the British by twenty-five to one.

The partnership between the two forces enabled the raider 'sand-screen' of the previous year to loom that much larger in the minds of the Italians and Germans, who were beginning to lose the psychological war in the desert.

CHEVROLET WA TRUCK

The Chevrolet truck which was used by the Long Range Desert Group. The SAS relied on LRDG teams for transportation to their targets. Later, they were to be equipped with their own vehicles.

ILLUSTRATION BY: JON WILKINSON

The Long Range Desert Group had managed to create a 'sand-screen' of movement in the Western Desert.

If the LRDG could pick the detachment up from a raid it might be able to take the SAS within walking distance of their target in the first place and thus avoid the considerable dangers of parachuting in unpredictable conditions. If another raid could be arranged quickly, the SAS might be able to attack again before MEHQ discovered the nature of their first abortive raid.

Explosives would have to be carried with time-pencils, as containers of each, once separated, would be of little use to the saboteurs. In the recent parachute-drop raid only Jock's men had been able to locate both containers.

David Stirling leans against a Chevrolet LRDG truck.

Captain David Lloyd Owen, discussed with Stirling and Lewes, the SAS' future prospects of transport, and between them it seems an agreement was reached whereby the LRDG generously provided the SAS with its 'taxi-service'. Jock and Stirling were also both fortunate because Brigadier John Marriott, ex-Guards Brigade, suggested that the SAS apply to Brigadier Denys Reid, who had only recently captured the Jalo garrison from the Italians. Reid, a giant of a man with a handshake to match, offered Jalo as the new SAS base. It was far from MEHQ and any unwanted attention; it also lay 150 miles south of Benghazi, in striking distance of the enemy airfields along the Gulf of Sirte. Both Reid's Flying Squadron and Marriott's force had already been ordered to link up in the area of Agedabia by 22 December, but there were German aircraft poised to attack any British troops at Agedabia, Sirte and Agheila. If Major Steele's LRDG squadron could operate as a 'taxi-service' for the SAS, then Lewes and Stirling could return a favour to both Marriott and Reid and reduce the threat of Axis planes targeting the Brigadiers' forces by attacking enemy aerodromes in the fortnight before.

To boost the men's morale the film of Auchinleck's visit to Kabrit was shown in the aerodrome cinema a fortnight after the abortive operation and a few days before their new posting. On 5 December the SAS flew out from Kabrit at 2.45 am and were in Jalo the same night. Jalo, in the Siwa Oasis, was about seven miles long and two miles wide with abundant water and a few palms. To the south of the dry heat and flies of Siwa lay the Great Sand Sea, a vast desert of huge dunes in a zone known as 'Devil's Country'. It lay within a desert that, including the Qattara Depression to the north-west, was approximately the size of India. The temperature ranges from 120 degrees Fahrenheit in the shade in June to 0 Fahrenheit in the bitterly cold winter nights. The skies afford no cloud cover during the heat of the day or after dark. In most of this area the population averages one person per square mile, and in one area of 100,000 square miles there is no one.

A few huts and Italian concrete camps were all that remained at Jalo, the indispensable centre of the Majabra Arabs who had once traded there. Johnny Cooper described it as '*a typical Foreign Legion outpost, straight out of* Beau Geste'. It was from here that the first phase of SAS raids began, with the LRDG initially acting as its parent unit. Before 22 Guards Brigade moved fifteen kilometres east of Benghazi in the last week of December, preliminary SAS raids would take place on 14 December against its prime objective of the Agedabia airfields on the Gulf of Sirte.

More raids would follow in the last days of December when the Allied assault on Benghazi reached its climax. Rommel was running out of fuel, and overstretched Axis supply lines would be vulnerable to attack. Driven by Gus Holliman and his Rhodesian LRDG patrol, Stirling and Mayne left for Sirte airfield 700km to the west of Jalo on 8 December in five ton pink and light green camouflaged lorries. Spotter planes were the greatest threat to the mission, and within a few kilometres of their destination they were bombed after a visit from a Gibli, an Italian reconnaissance plane. Stirling had been leading a group of eleven men, the standard sub-unit that he had up to then agreed with Lewes to take on such operations. Since they had been observed by the enemy, Stirling split his force into two and directed Blair Mayne to lead his men in an assault on Tamit, thirty miles away.

It is possible that from this time the idea of the substantially smaller SAS sub-unit was born, because in the circumstances it not only made sense to avoid jeopardizing the whole raid by keeping the men together after the Gibli sighting, it also increased the probability that more enemy aircraft would be located. With Lewes Bombs weighing so little, it required only a few men to carry and attach up to fifty on the entire target area. Each group of six men could then destroy an airfield.

Stirling's gambit paid off, because, although his half of the soldiers had entered a minefield that resulted in an abortive raid on Sirte, twenty-four planes had been destroyed at Tamit by the other six men. The control panel of the last plane at Tamit has become part of SAS folklore because Blair Mayne had run out of Lewes Bombs and used his bare hands to disable the aircraft. On their first active raid the six SAS men had blown up half as many planes as the whole of Fighter Command on their most successful day during the Battle of Britain.

The concept of a five or four-man patrol, which the SAS later adopted, gained credence, particularly after Blair Mayne's success.

Jock headed north-east into enemy territory on 8 December with eleven of his own men and Lieutenant Morris' LRDG party. Their objective was the landing ground at Agheila where they hoped to bag a whole airfield. By night they had covered 120 miles on level sand and were only ten miles south-east of Benghazi. In daylight the going was rough with steep hills and rocky ridges, but the terrain, with its gazelles and herds of wild animals, broke the monotony. Two days after setting out they camped thirteen miles from their target area. Jim Almonds camouflaged the lorries after he and Jock had patrolled near the main road. Then Jock, with ten men, positioned himself by Agheila aerodrome, hiding until 13 December. The airfield was deserted and Jock blew up a mile of telegraph wire and several lorries along the Tripoli road, and brought in 'Sambo', a dusky Italian corporal, as his prisoner. Sambo had left part of his platoon behind – the rest of the Italians were all disappointed when he was the only one taken along as prisoner.

Before arriving at Agheila, Jock and Jim Almonds had insisted on bringing a captured Italian Lancia lorry with them, much to the chagrin of the rest of the men. It had always been his intention to use the Lancia behind enemy lines as a ruse to deceive the enemy. Now the opportunity presented itself. There was an Italian station house nearby which could be entered using the Lancia. With Lady Luck sitting on the men's shoulders, it might well pass through any German or Italian road block. The Italian lorry unfortunately had a tendency to sink into the desert sands and break down more often than any other vehicle which Jock's men travelled in. Reg Seekings remembered it was '*the bane of my life starting the engine with a crankshaft that only I could turn on my own*'. Before reaching Agheila the usefulness of the Lancia was not apparent, but now Jock and Jim held the

The Special Air Service 'taxi service': vehicles and drivers of the Long Range Desert Group await the the order to go.

vehicle as a trump card with which to turn disaster into triumph.

At dusk on 14 December Jock and his party travelled in more comfort on well-made Italian roads in order to find the staging post at Mersa Brega. Enemy traffic was busy on the Tripoli road, travelling in fleets of about ten vehicles. In the Lancia Jock led a shorter column with five LRDG cars behind; the Lancia had no working lights but Lieutenant Morris' lorry shone full headlights onto the Italian truck. The SAS convoy was relatively inconspicuous, despite passing within a foot of the enemy on the other side of the narrow track.

The plan was to attack the Mersa Brega roadhouse at night and destroy as many vehicles as possible, but all this was timed to happen after Jock targeted the roadhouse itself, which was known to sometimes accommodate senior officers. Jock hoped to capture some VIP prisoners to join 'Sambo', since the latter had not been a mine of information. He had always instructed his men to act naturally when raiding behind enemy lines, as their light khaki uniforms would lend credence to their likeness to Axis troops; this was essential as Jim Almonds recalled that the SAS passed no less than forty-seven enemy vehicles.

The raiders were 'in the best of spirits': some sat on the top of their vehicles, lit up cigarettes, smiled and waved at the streams of Italian and German lorry drivers travelling in the opposite direction. About midnight they reached a turning where a track led to the roadhouse, around which were parked twenty or more cars with their German and Italian crews, some of whom were waiting for a meal. Jock parked his own Lancia next to a number of others. The Breda machine gun on the back was primed and made ready.

Alongside Jock's lorry an Italian driver got out of his Lancia and asked for a light, which Jock gave him. Pranks played against the enemy were undertaken with all seriousness. Captain Derrick Harrison in his memoir, *These Men Are Dangerous*, describes Jock's audacity:

'*Got a light?*' the Italian asked. Lewes flicked open his lighter and held it to him. '*Suppose you have guessed that we are English.*' '*Eh?*' replied the Italian. '*We are English – Inglesi!*' Jock said.

He threw back his head and laughed, '*You Germans have such a wonderful sense of humour,*' he said. He began to walk over to the resthouse. '*Come here*' ordered Lewes.

The driver stopped and turned. The cigarette fell from his lips. Lewes was pointing a revolver at him. '*Get in*' said Lewes, nodding towards the back of the lorry.

Jock hustled him around the back of his own truck where the Italian went silent and then '*broke down and cried like a child*'; hands were placed over his mouth to stop him '*spoiling the show*'. The lorry was driven fifty yards to give sufficient room to operate the machine gun, but Jim Almonds found to his horror that the oil in the Breda MG had congealed in the cold night air. Armed with Thompson machine guns and revolvers, the SAS party planted thirty-eight Lewes Bombs on the surrounding cars. Then a 'sharp fight started' as the

Sergeant Rose and Jimmie Storie, two original SAS troopers.

enemy recovered from their surprise, sheltering in the buildings around which they closed their gates. Enemy fire was poor and erratic and this enabled the SAS to get away and move down the road without any casualties. Charges were placed on more telegraph poles, and after several miles Corporal Garven of the LRDG laid a few mines in the road before the convoy left it for a safe place to camouflage the trucks and lay up during the day. Their prisoner got drunk on rum and sang long into a night that was also punctuated by the reports of at least seven more explosions in Mersa Brega.

By 18 December Jock was back in Jalo to discover that, although Stirling had found a deserted enemy airfield at Sirte, the planes had taken off to land in what was considered to be the relative security of Tamil. However, Blair Mayne had been successful in destroying the twenty-four enemy aeroplanes that landed there. The next day Lieutenant Fraser left with five men to attack Agedabia and was back two days later with the news that thirty-seven enemy planes had been destroyed. Two SAS men had been killed, but all Jock and Stirling's ideas had been vindicated in two weeks of fighting. Brigadier Reid's and Marriott's gambit of offering Jalo to the SAS had paid off handsomely.

Jock had little time to rest because on Christmas Eve he prepared for a new raid. Stirling and Lewes wanted to silence the doubters of the 'new learning' at MEHQ, so it was hoped that another significant strike was worth attempting before the SAS contacted Cairo in the New Year. Rommel was retreating and would need all the available air cover for his withdrawal, so any reduction in the number of enemy planes would markedly increase the SAS' military credibility. The Germans were already becoming wise to the raids and salvaging wreckage from one plane to rebuild another, so the SAS placed their Lewes Bombs on left wings only to frustrate the enemy who were forced to wait for new replacements.

Jock left for Nofilia aerodrome early on Christmas

morning, a day after Stirling and Mayne called the enemy's bluff by raiding Sirte and Tamit for the second time in a fortnight. Jim Almond's diary records how Jock and Lieutenant Fraser proceeded towards Marble Arch and Nofilia airfields. Jock and his men watched Stukas alighting and taking off from their bases on 28 December, when the party left their lorries and walked the eighteen miles to the outskirts of their target.

At 2.00 am on 29 December Jock's party was within a few miles of their target, but the men were forced to make a few detours around escarpments used by Axis troops. The men covered themselves with sand and shrubs for, as Dr Pleydell, the SAS doctor, later remarked,

> 'There is no lesson which improves camou-flage as well as a low level machine-gunning attack.' Jim Almonds wrote, 'Hope we don't wake up to find ourselves in someone's barrack square.'

When they did wake, it was to the roar of brand new, brightly painted Stukas; the group observed forty-three planes on the drome. They watched the activity and planned the campaign for that almost fully moonlit night. 'Jock thought we were going to have a real harvest.' However, all the Stukas took off and the only targets left were two out-of-service planes which they promptly destroyed.

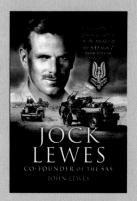

The original SAS parachute insignia which could be worn after three operations behind enemy lines.

In early December Jock had informed his parents that 'L' Detachment had achieved full Brigade status, *'after all you can't go on being a detachment all your life'.* He also sent home,

> 'Our wings... an arrogant badge for you to see and imagine on my breast. They are earned only after long training has achieved its purpose in operation.'

That insignia was the precursor of Sergeant Tait's Wings and Sword insignia with its motto *'Who Dares Wins'.* The right to wear Jock's original parachute badge was earned after parachutists achieved three operations behind enemy lines. Regarding the origin of the wings design, which have an Egyptian appearance, Jock had noticed the outstretched wings of the symbolic Ibis in the foyer at Shepheard's Hotel; he removed the Ibis and substituted a parachute. The two shades of blue have reference to Jock's affiliation with Oxford, dark blue, and the light blue for Cambridge – in deference to another SAS officer, Tommy Langton, who had rowed against Oxford in the Boat Race of 1937. It is not surprising that the leader who by then had left his mark on almost every aspect of the SAS' character should also want to design its insignia. The parachute in the parachutists' badge had come to symbolize much of Jock's work in North Africa.

END OF A LIVING LEGEND

It was no raid like that at Mersa Brega which uplifted the men's spirits; no roadhouse target within striking distance before they travelled north-west to pick up Lieutenant Fraser.

At 10.00 am on 31 December a lone Messerschmitt 110 fighter with armed with four machine guns and two cannons passed overhead and appeared to go away. Jim Almonds noted that, *'everyone breathed a sigh of relief'.* The men were more than ready for their journey back to Jalo, a clean-up and news from loved ones. Then, in the distance, it was noted that one wing tipped down and the pilot brought the machine round and began circling getting nearer. Then, suddenly the Messerschmitt began a low-level attack. Jimmie Storie remembered the hole down the middle of one of the trucks through which they quickly evacuated. There began a deadly game of 'ring-a-ring-o-roses' around a cluster of rocks as men sought cover each time the plane circled and attacked.

Jim Almonds recorded that Jock had been wounded in the leg. It was Jimmie Storie who came upon Jock lying on the ground – his back blown out by a 20mm cannon shell. Stone, who had trained with Jock from the inception of the parachute detachment, was the last to see him as he buried him in the desert. With no other casualties the men managed to salvage the pieces of one truck and limp back to Jalo.

'The green Very light went up and we wound slowly like a snake, firing at the aircraft as we went. Clouds obscured the moon, and one after another the planes burst into flames, but not a gun was fired on us. We fired into their huts and tents, and we could see one or two figures running helplessly about.'

PROVING ITS WORTH

With David Stirling a new idea was born. It was to strike at the enemy's exposed line of communication from deep inside the desert. At first he suffered setbacks, in that 'air drops' had proved disastrous, resulting in the death of his closest lieutenant, Jock Lewes. The LRDG came to the aid of Stirling as a kind of drop-and-carry desert taxi service. However, the SAS was about to have its own transport and navigators.

By Carol Mather

This article was extracted from *When the Grass Stops Growing* and is reproduced by permission of Pen & Sword Books Ltd.

The activity at Kabrit, a tented camp alongside the Canal, was frantic. Here I met many old soldiers from No 8 Commando, whom David had recruited, so in a way it was like returning home. The ubiquitous American jeep had arrived for the first time in the Middle East. David had managed to grab the first batch. We spent most of our time between the Base Ordnance Depot drawing the vehicles and Base Workshops seeing to their modification. These were the first vehicles seen in the Middle East with four-wheel drive – an immense improvement for crossing sandy terrain, tough, versatile and with a decent mileage to the gallon. Two men and their kit was the payload; for operations we could put an extra man in the back.

The Camp was comfortable for had it not been established by those very tactics which we were now to follow, 'hit and run raids' on neighbouring camps? Our New Zealander neighbours were to discover that many of their tents had disappeared mysteriously during the night.

Within two weeks of my arrival we were off! Our next operation was to raid enemy airfields immediately behind the German lines. This was to be the first SAS (then known as L Detachment) operation with its own transport and navigators. We used jeeps newly mounted with machine guns, and three-ton trucks to carry all our supplies of fuel, food, ammunition and explosives. Our party amounted to ten officers and 100 men.

It was now June, 1942. After the fall of Tobruk, 8th Army had retired to the Alamein Line, the final stand before Alexandria and the Nile Delta, which was only sixty miles away. In case of defeat at Alamein, and defeatism was in the air, we carried maps which would enable our party to escape south-west to Lake Chad in French Equatorial Africa, via the oasis of Kufra, south to the Sudan, or east into Sinai and the Levant, as the situation demanded.

'Within two weeks of my arrival we were off! Our next operation was to raid enemy airfields immediately behind the German lines. This was to be the first SAS operation with its own transport and navigators.'

Two photographs showing the various armaments fitted to the Willys jeeps. Above left: the passenger mans the .50 calibre Browning machine gun.

Travelling west from 8th Army HQ from the Alexandria-Cairo Road, we passed north of Wadi Natrun reaching the base of the Alamein line after a day's journey. Having passed safely through the line we hugged the lip of the Qattara Depression following occasionally an indistinct track marked by palm leaves. The bottom of the Depression could not be seen, only a descending series of cliffs and boulders dropping sharply until their outline was lost in a shimmer of pink. A further two days' travelling brought us to a point about thirty miles north of the Qattara Spring, fifty miles from

the enemy-controlled coast at Mersa Matruh and one hundred miles due west of the Alamein line. Here was a long low escarpment which offered good cover for our thirty vehicles, and this we formed as our base for operations.

For fourteen days and nights we attacked almost every night the airfields lying between Daba and Mersa Matruh or other opportunity targets. Our tactics were to drive as close as we could to the enemy airfield and then walk round the dispersed aircraft and place a time-bomb in the cockpit or on the wing. At that stage of mobile

THE SAS WILLYS JEEP

The Willys jeep was heavily armed with a .50 calibre Browning and three Vickers K machine guns. The firepower was a variation of ball, armour-piercing and tracer rounds, ideal for destroying parked enemy aircraft. A single jeep was capable of delivering 5000 rounds per minute.

ILLUSTRATION BY: JON WILKINSON

warfare, with the constant moving of forward airfields, the enemy had not the means of establishing proper airfield defence and the planes were seldom guarded; neither were the cockpits locked.

George Jellicoe, Stephen Hastings and I, departing on one of these operations, were detected by enemy aircraft and got properly strafed, losing two of our three vehicles. The remaining jeep was holed in the radiator, its tyres slashed and the vehicle resting only on its wheel hubs, but the engine still running. We made the thirty mile journey back to base with nine men up. A bright idea led us to plug the holed radiator with plastic explosive from our unused bombs. For water we relied on mother nature. Each man would relieve himself into the radiator in turn. It worked! But it smelt like a chicken coop!

These constant night operations took their toll, for those who were called upon nightly began to suffer from a drastic loss of sleep. It was impossible to sleep, except for a fitful doze, by day because of the heat and flies. At night we were always on the move or on operations. In the last days of the fortnight we had become a party of sleepwalkers, with men dropping off at the wheel or on their feet. Not an ideal way of sending an army into battle! This does not mean that blame attached to Stirling. We were all in this together and all of an equal mind, both officers and men. But Stirling was the natural leader in daring, imagination and execution of the plan, and most important of all, we were actually winning our private war against a ruthless and efficient enemy. Stirling was proving a dynamic leader, gone were the days of lethargy and idleness. His leadership technique was a peculiarly gentle one with a diffident and charming manner which made many of his more audacious exploits difficult to resist. Some of these plans had the element of a huge practical joke played upon the Axis forces, so unexpected were the attacks and so helpless and confused their reaction.

After two weeks of such operations, supplies and vehicles began to run out and had to be replenished. Several of our jeeps had been damaged or lost in air attacks. David decided to leave a small retaining force at the Escarpment Rendezvous, Stephen Hastings, myself and the Medical Officer Malcolm Pleydell a total of thirty officers and men; the remainder returned with all speed to Cairo. A fast party under Stirling managed to force their way down the camel track at the Qattara Spring, drop into the Depression and reach Cairo in two days. The heavy party travelling on top of the escarpment filtered through the base of the Alamein line and reached

The author behind twin Vickers machine guns. Fellow officer, Gordon Alston is behind the wheel. The American Jeep was the ideal mount for the new unit.

Cairo intact in three days.

Two hectic days were spent in Cairo refitting and collecting new vehicles, and then the new force of about twenty-five jeeps returned by way of the Qattara Depression.

It was an eerie experience once the others had departed. Silence descended upon the desert, the heat clamped down upon us as we lay as if stunned in the comparative cool and security of our caves. We banned all movement by day, and the twilight hour we spent removing telltale tracks round our hideout. At that stage we had no idea whether Stirling's group would ever

Constant night operations took their toll on the patrol teams, leaving men exhausted and unable to catch up on sleep during the heat of the sun.

reach Cairo, when they might return, or what action we should take if surprised.

Stephen Hastings and I shared a cave. He was another recent recruit. He had come from the 2nd Scots Guards and had spent a year with his battalion in the Western Desert. The role of an infantry officer in this kind of mobile warfare was not an enviable one.

Steve and I, in one of those brief wartime relationships, got to know each other very well, and then we parted, never to meet again for the rest of the war. His companionship was one of those unexpected wartime bonuses. He was an incurable romantic, his Scots ancestry having bitten deep into his psyche. His repertoire of ballad and song, including of course a rendering of the sentimental but haunting 'Lili Marlene', kept our spirits up. Another bonus was his knowledge of and sympathy with the French. A section of Free French soldiers accompanied us and enlivened our operations. Among the names I remember were Le Grand, Zirnhold, Martin, Harent and Klein.

We took it in turns to keep watch, on a vantage point above our cave, where the dust devils and mirages played games with the imagination. Hostile aircraft were about, but they never spotted our location.

In the early morning Steve and I would walk down from the French cave, which was at best a pile of boulders, to our 'daytime cave' near the cookhouse. Here we would spend the remainder of the day. It was a long and low grotto with a floor of soft white sand. At one end a great lip curved over, touching the ground and forming a cool enclosed space, whilst at the extreme end grew a stunted palm. At best it would only contain three men lying down, but there was just room for a mosquito net to be suspended from the eaves which covered us quite easily. Once in it was a question of exterminating the flies and settling down to some of the unsuitable books which we carried, Thackeray's *The Virginians*, Lawrence's *Seven Pillars of Wisdom*, or Hemingway's *For Whom the Bell Tolls*,.Above our heads were embedded a variety of marine fossils and shells and we had the leisure to consider in what strange manner they had arrived there.

But for the most part we let our imaginations run riot upon the theme of 'the ideal day in Cairo'. This became a kind of castle-in-the-air, combining every luxury and diversion that the mind could conceive. It became known as 'Comforts Day' and whiled away the interminable hours.

Our tranquility was disturbed twice. Shortly after the main party had left for Cairo, the navigator of Robin Gurdon's LRDG patrol, Tinker, which had been operating in the coastal area, flopped down in our cave. He had been an officer in the Merchant Navy and was an expert navigator. He always wore a little white Arab skull cap and was a calm and reliable man. On this occasion he was badly shaken as he told us that Gurdon

'As the enemy was now getting wise to our walk-on tactics, for the next operation David planned a mass attack on an aerodrome using our full armament.'

has been killed and one man badly wounded by strafing. He blamed himself because he had missed our hideout and had spent several valuable hours in searching for it, during which Gurdon had died. After that there had been an argument in the patrol as to the course they should follow, which he knew was the wrong one.

We hurriedly dug a grave down in the flat, and Pleydell took the wounded man into his expert hands. A few days after this an LRDG officer who had been out on a watching patrol at Sidi Barrani came tearing in with stories that there were German patrols in our area, which had already been chasing him. This proved untrue and we sent him off with the wounded man and the officer-less LRDG patrol to Cairo.

After eight days our food and water situation was serious and we began to get anxious about our fate, so we were relieved to hear a great rattling on the escarpment above and to see thirty brand new jeeps coming bumping down, complete with fresh crews and four Vickers (K) to each vehicle. David stumbled into our grotto bearing a pint jar of eau de Cologne, Turkish delight, cigars, tobacco, new pipes and an exhaustive store of plans for the future.

There was much rejoicing as we greeted parted companions, and even more rejoicing over the goodies they had brought. Nothing had changed in their absence. Here we were, still undetected, approximately 100 miles behind the enemy's lines, and 30 miles from the coast, but all the new kit and equipment David had brought and his dashing plans for the future changed our outlook completely.

As the enemy was now getting wise to our walk-on tactics, for the next operation David planned a mass attack on an aerodrome using our full armament. This consisted of two pairs of twin Vickers (K) machine guns (as used by the RAF) per jeep. With fifteen jeeps earmarked for this operation, it made a total of sixty machine guns, a formidable firepower.

The question was, which aerodrome? Our 11 set was kept busy with reports from 8th Army HQ on the present use of enemy airfields, but such reports were so confusing that David became exasperated. He sent a strongly worded signal back to Army HQ which unfortunately fell into the hands of the new Army Commander, General Montgomery, instead of General Auchinleck for whom it had been intended. The peppery general was not amused by these threats from 'the Boy David' whom he had never heard of before.

George Jellicoe, Sandy Scratchley and Paddy Mayne, my companions on the previous operations, had returned with the reinforcements. Also Chris Bailey, a most useful man who had kept an inn in Cyprus before the war with a renowned kitchen. He had transferred from the Cyprus Mule Company to the 4th Hussars and had just spent a year at 8th Army headquarters, so that his advice was invaluable.

George Jellicoe, following our abortive raid from Tobruk, had just carried out a daring raid on an aerodrome on the north coast of Crete. He and a party of French had been landed by submarine, had destroyed nineteen German aircraft, had made their way across the island to the south coast, where according to a pre-determined plan they had been picked up by a caique.

David Russell, who had recently arrived in Egypt with a Scots Guards draft, also joined us. I described him as '*a wild and independent character with a zest for life, but better at giving orders than taking them!*' The new intake was completed by an RAF liaison officer named Pike who was there to help with air supply. He had followed the almost irreplaceable Derek Raumsley whom everyone loved. Pike, an Australian, proved a worthy successor. He was deeply impressed by our aircraft score and could not get over the sudden departures armed to the teeth, and a few days later the arrivals back, waterless and on foot. Such a reaction boosted our morale, ever a sensitive emotion.

It became apparent that the most likely airfield to attack was LG 21 at Fuka, fifty miles away near the coast. There was one day for preparation and rehearsal. We had discovered a new cave about a mile up the escarpment. It was long and low and in it we could fit twenty jeeps side by side. When they were all safely stowed away we hung camou flage nets from the overhanging lip of the cave right down to the ground. Thus we were completely invisible.

The cave, I wrote, rather reminded me of the scene in the film *Snow White and the Seven Dwarfs.*

There was much hammering and clattering and singing as new wheels and tyres were fitted. The Vickers guns were stripped and cleaned, magazines loaded, engines taken down, and explosives made up. At one end of the cave two four-gallon petrol cans containing bully

stew were sizzling over a large fire. At the other David was poring over maps and figures. George (who was in charge of the commissariat) was, with a great tin of acid drops in front of him, trying to work out the impossible problems of supply. Paddy, fast asleep and unrecognizable entwined under a large mosquito net, with his head under one jeep and his feet under another. All around in the soft sand lay tins of tobacco, sweets, pipes, jars of eau de Cologne (there was no water for washing), and last year's glossy magazines. George had thoughtfully spent £20 in Cairo on these luxuries, (£150 in today's currency) for which he would never be repaid. His characteristic mixture of ebullience and level-headedness were a great addition to our party.

That same evening, 20 July, we carried out our dress rehearsal. We drove out into the plain as the light faded, formed up into two columns of seven jeeps each, with our leader, David, at the head and centre. We were fifteen jeeps all told, each jeep, as planned, mounted with four Vickers (K) guns, with two gunners and a driver. The officer drove the vehicle in order to control his lethal machine, and taking care, in my case, not to lean forward or backwards into the line of fire. The magazines of our sixty guns contained a mixture of ball, armour-piercing, tracer and incendiary bullets. We practised forming line abreast and line astern, opening fire on David's green Very Signal and following exactly in the tracks of the leaders, for each gun was firing outwards. When we opened up the noise was deafening, but, apart from one French jeep running amok, the practice was successful. We now only had to get there.

MASS ATTACK

The following day we continued with our loading, everything we would need for that night's operation. In particular the stowage of spare ammunition drums

SAS RAIDS ON ENEMY TARGETS

KEY
➡ Allied forces
SAS raids

CRETE

MEDITERRANEAN SEA

Tripoli

Barce Slonta
Benina Derna
Benghazi Tmimi
Berca Tobruk
Bouerat Tamet Gazala Bardia Mersa Matruh Alexandria
Sirte Bagush
Nofilia Agedabia Fuka
El Aghelia Sidi Haneish

EL ALAMEIN LINE

Cairo

CYRENAICA

LIBYA GIALO OASIS SIWA OASIS EGYPT
Gialo QATTARA DEPRESSION NILE
GREAT SAND SEA

which had to be within ready reach. Of course we were overloaded, we always were, and this took its toll on tyres, springs and sometimes sumps. A sump could split open like a ripe melon, spilling its contents on the sand, if at night one hit an unseen rock.

We left the escarpment RV at last light and climbed up the rocky cliff in our two columns. There was a full moon and so driving was comparatively easy. David led off at a terrific speed and it was not long before we were suffering from punctures. We had fifteen before we reached our objective, and for each one a halt of five minutes had to be made. One jeep and its crew had to be abandoned on the way owing to a cracked sump, and at this halt David gave us our final instructions;

'Right lads, we haven't got much time. At the edge of the aerodrome form a line abreast and all guns spray the area. When I advance follow me in your two columns and on my green Very light open fire, outwards at the aircraft – follow exactly in each other's tracks, five yards apart – speed not more than 4 mph. Return to the RV independently moving only by night.'

He spoke casually as if putting us into our butts for a grouse drive.

Michael Sadler, a young Rhodesian from the LRDG, was navigating. After fifty miles and three compass legs we hit the target off exactly. But what with the breakdowns we were rather late and had only two hours left before dawn. We descended across an old battlefield, where some of our corpses were lying still unburied, in the full moonlight. The burnt-out tanks and corpses looked cold and comfortless, and I took another swig of rum. Then we heard an aircraft overhead – it was circling low. Suddenly all the aerodrome landing lights were switched on and we saw our target perfectly illuminated, and the German bomber came in to land. The noise of its engines drowned our own. A hundred yards more to the aerodrome edge and we formed line abreast, halted and suddenly fired our sixty guns. A minute's fire to spray the defences and then we followed David in our two columns. In one minute we were amongst the parked aircraft – Messerschmitts, Stukas, Junkers and Heinkels lay all around us. The green Very light went up and we wound slowly like a snake, firing at the aircraft as we went. Clouds obscured the moon, and one after another the planes burst into flames, but not a gun was fired on us. We fired into their huts and tents, and we could see one or two figures running helplessly about. Some of the aircraft would only be fifteen yards away, and as I passed them at the end of the column they would glow red and explode with a deafening 'phut' and there would be great heat.

We had passed through the dispersal area, and were swinging round for a second visit, when an Ack Ack gun some 300 yards away opened up on us wildly. Our port-side guns returned the fire, but the German gunner had

hit one of our jeeps in the centre of the column as we drew away, the shots passing over our heads. Then we stopped:

'Switch off!', came the cry. We were still in the middle of the aerodrome, but there was dead silence. Then,

'Anybody hurt? Are you OK? Any ammunition left?'

'Only one drum!' came from somewhere.

'Any ammunition? Any ammunition?' went echoing down the line, then,

'OK. We're going to start off now. Start up!'

And the cry went back down the line, *'Start up! Start up! Start up!'*

As we moved off the aerodrome Paddy Mayne spotted an untouched bomber and, jumping from his jeep with a bomb in his hand, ran up to it and, placing the bomb in its engine, ran back and caught us up.

We had burnt thirty aircraft, damaged more, and lost one jeep and one man, a Frenchman, killed. The whole thing had taken fifteen minutes. Then we melted into the desert in twos and threes, as arranged.

I stopped to have a look at the party. Three jeeps, two of which had irreparable punctures, eight men and one wounded. There was about 1½ hours' darkness left, then the sun would rise and we must seek cover for the day. We drove very fast watching the stars for our direction, and watching for that paleness to appear which meant dawn. I wanted, if possible, to cross the telegraph track before light, but I didn't want to stop anywhere near it. The stars paled and the dawn came, and with it a blessing. A great white blanket of mist engulfed us so that we were able to continue driving unseen. As the sun rose the mist lifted, and there, only a few hundred yards away was the telegraph track. We became fearful of aircraft but took the risk and tore down the track on our tyreless rims bumping and rattling over the rocky surface until we came to three stones placed in a triangle which had been put there the night before to serve as a guide for our return. Here we swung west on a bearing 320 degrees trying to put a mile or two between us and the track. Running parallel with us to our south was a long low escarpment, which offered good cover. To our front was short and patchy scrub. The escarpment might be dangerous, so we found a patch of camel thorn rising not more than a foot – dispersed our vehicles amongst it and camouflaged up.

We felt very bare and exposed in this spot, but decided to revive our spirits with a little breakfast.

No sooner had the tea come up to a boil and the sausages started sizzling than the first aircraft appeared. 'Aircraft,' someone said in that quiet and urgent voice which we had learnt to dread, and we all froze whilst it passed harmlessly over – a Stuka weaving and searching its way down the long low escarpment. I told the men to scatter themselves 400 yards away from the vehicles and not to move, put a few finishing touches to the camouflage, sorrowfully left the breakfast and then walked slowly away myself looking over my shoulder for aeroplanes and stopping and listening every few

> 'At the edge of the aerodrome form a line abreast and all guns spray the area.'

paces. I took a rough bearing on where we had left the jeeps and then chose a meagre bush, which seemed to rise almost eighteen inches, spread my handkerchief over two of its twigs and lay my head on the piece of ground on which the shadow was cast.

Soon the sky became alive with aircraft circling angrily round and round, like a swarm of angry bees, out to seek vengeance on the destruction of the night before. We got no shelter from the July sun, and we could not visit the vehicles for food or water, and so we lay counting the minutes and watching the sun creep across the sky. We could see fires in the distance and watched Stukas dive again and again at unseen targets and the

black smoke curl angrily up across the horizon. Our position was so exposed that although the aircraft flew directly over us, they never spotted our vehicles – searching instead into the shadows of the escarpment and into the rougher ground to our north.

After twelve hours of terrific heat, the sun seemed to lose its intensity and quickly sank below the horizon in the direction that we must follow.

We waited for another fifteen minutes as the darkness fell upon us. Our spirits began to rise and our bodies glow with the stimulant of a day's exposure to the sun. After a short search we found our jeeps, lit a fire for a cup of char and stew, changed the wheel hubs upon

Some aircraft types that would never support Rommel's Afrika Korps again. In order to render cannibalising more difficult, SAS raiders began attaching Lewes bombs to left wings only.

Top; Junkers 88.
Middle; Messerschmitt 109
Below; Junkers 87 dive bomber

which we had been running for new ones, then squatted down in the sand around the fire with our mess tins in front of us. We ate in silence.

The eight young men in the circle around the fire were already veterans. Corporal Lily, a Coldstreamer from commando days, stared in silence at his empty mess tin. He wore a head cloth tied pirate-fashion round his forehead, he had a long drooping moustache and a black beard. How splendidly those pre-war guardsmen stood up to this irregular warfare, I thought. Lily was a bit of a philosopher and had a motherly streak. He was concerned for the wounded men, and young Dalziel (one of my former commando lads), and for the rest of us, I do believe, from the fatalistic expression on his face.

Corporal Lambie was with me again, always a steady and uncomplaining man. The others I did not know so well, but they were all desert-hardened, understanding how to use those unpromising elements, the sun, the moon and the stars to best advantage. So we were a silent circle, each brooding on his own thoughts, resting for an hour until the moon had changed from orange to silver, and the desert had been flooded with a light almost as bright as day.

We threw off the camouflage nets, filled up with petrol and water and put the wounded man in an easy position in the back of one of the jeeps. Then I walked out with my compass and took a bearing of 320 degrees and found a corresponding constellation of stars, on which we could drive. It should only be a matter of eighteen miles to the escarpment RV. It should also be easy to find because we couldn't miss the escarpment, and once we had found it, it was only a question of turning right or left until we came upon our people. Luckily we found our tracks of the previous evening so that now we knew we were right. They were quite easy to follow until suddenly we lost them completely and so continued on our old bearing.

After thirteen miles we were a little surprised to arrive at our escarpment, at least it looked like our escarpment as there were hundreds of jeep and 3-tonner tracks running in all directions. And there also were the wadis up which the vehicles had been run and camouflaged. And yet it was deserted and not quite the same. We got out and examined the tracks closely – they couldn't have been a day old. How very mysterious! Perhaps we were too far down. So we drove up the cliffside for three miles and down it for three miles and saw not a sign of life. It was the same escarpment and yet it wasn't the same escarpment – not quite the same. It was deserted. Could they have all moved away and left no one to pick us up?

As soon as we had stopped, all the men except Corporal Lily and myself had nodded and dropped off to sleep, and so we thought quietly for a few minutes and then decided to drive on for five miles further. That distance would tally with our milometer reading. And

'Another party had shot down a Stuka and had captured the airman who turned out to be one of Rommel's personal pilots, and a German doctor who was also in the plane.'

yet we couldn't understand why they had left our escarpment, because it was our escarpment in almost every detail, and if it wasn't, why all the jeep and three tonner tracks? It was a mystery which was not attractive at three o'clock in the morning. All the usual uneasy feelings began to creep into the back of my mind. Supposing we are lost, and our petrol gives out – which it will do after a few more miles; and then the wounded man – he won't be able to walk. But then fatigue came to the rescue. To concentrate on driving and watching the stars was enough – there was no room for hopes or fears. And then there was always only one answer to these kind of vital problems, and now it was to drive for five miles, to stop and wait for the morning. Tomorrow could take care of itself. We pulled up after five miles in a small depression, and then suddenly, light of heart, we unstrapped our bedding, laid it out on the sand and slept.

After an hour I awoke, roused my gunner, Lambie, and walked over to Lily's jeep and told him I was going to reconnoitre. Dawn was coming with a heavy mist and we got into the jeep, left the bedding on the ground and drove straight towards the moon which was on the exact line of our bearing. It was low in the sky and turning pink, and I was just saying to Lambie how fortunate it was, now the stars had gone in, that we had the moon to drive on, when suddenly through the mist we saw a drop and there was a cairn.

I could recognize every stone of the cairn, it was the one that Steve and I had spent many weary hours watching from in the scorching sun. Yes, it must be the same one. And there, there was one of the three tonner bays – a small wadi where we left the explosives. And there, my god, was a real and solid 3-tonner draped in its camouflage net. I was right the whole time and my bearing and distances were dead correct. Why had I ever showed the men that I doubted? I told Lambie casually that I thought we were about right and didn't show my excitement, and a great smile spread over his face. We drove the half mile back to the others, shouted, 'Wake up, we're home, come on, pack up and get the engines started'. Then we dropped down the cliff over the familiar bumps and along the cliff edge, stirring up great clouds of talcum powder dust until we reached the long cave, and then up and into it with the three jeeps making thunder in its eaves and waking the sleepers on the ground.

We were the first home, but then, as day came, first one and then another battered jeep came rolling in. David and George and Steve and six men arrived on one jeep grinding along on four buckled wheel hubs. They too had thought they were lost and had evidently stumbled across the same false escarpment as we had. They, for an awful moment, had thought that it was the coastal escarpment, that their compass was wrong and that the sea lay beyond. One of the French officers had been killed by the strafing of the day before. Another party had shot down a Stuka and had captured the airman who turned out to be one of Rommel's personal pilots, and a German doctor who was also in the plane.

We thought it rather odd that he should be riding about in a German dive-bomber for no reason at all. For all he could say was, '*I went up for plissure, but it ended unheppily*'. These and other remarks, about his pre-war visit to 'Clicton-on-Sea', caused us intense amusement, light-headed as we were after the excitement of thirty enemy aircraft destroyed, one Stuka shot down, two prisoners, and all of us back safely except two. And there was the unforgettable exhilaration of a cool clean morning in the desert after a night of nightmare quality.

In the sober heat of the day we lay flat on our backs pestered by the flies and hoping terribly that we could get some rest at last. But no, tonight we must move further south and west because the enemy would do everything he could to find us now. And this RV.

We had used it for over twenty days in the most blatant fashion; it was one hundred miles behind the enemy lines and only thirty from the nearest point on the coast. Clearly it was wiser for us to be gone, and as soon as we could. And then there was something else. I was warned to leave immediately on a six-day operation to strafe enemy vehicles immediately behind their lines. And there was one other thing. A half-dismantled jeep had been left by the Frenchman's grave fifteen miles away on which there were some valuable spares, which somebody had to go and get – someone who knew how to navigate, like Steve or me.

David, Steve and myself lay in the doctor's cave. We were waiting our turn. Someone was going to be fagged to do this chore. One of us had to go. It was either Steve or me. David said slowly, '*Carol, no, Steve, will you go and collect those spares?*' I thought, '*Thank God for that, poor old Steve.*' He was in an almost worse condition than myself and shortly he was to fall seriously sick. Stephen had not returned by nightfall. George and I went up to the escarpment top to give him a lead in with a burst of Vickers. Our nerves were so shattered that we could not stand any more of that rat-tat-tat, and fired off a Very light instead. No sign of him, so, being now ready to move, we left a jeep and two men behind to pick him up.

Shortly after midnight our convoy of twenty-five vehicles left on a westward bearing. This was our third successive night without sleep and it was a weary drive. I was sharing a jeep with George. I was driving first, whilst he slept. It was a beautiful night, the desert so soft and silvery, under the clear light of the moon, the stars so big and brilliant and the sky so deep blue. Adjusting to another sleepless night I was almost reluctant for George to take over at half way. Our little convoy spread across thirty miles of desert during the night (no lights of course). Half an hour before dawn we halted, we were missing ten vehicles. I followed the tracks back the way we had come for five miles and found the little group halted in their tracks, every man fast asleep. It took me all of ten minutes to wake them all, and by the time we

had rejoined the others they were already moving off to some nearby broken ground where we would form our new RV.

Having dispersed the vehicles amongst the wadis and scrub and devoured an enormous breakfast, we all tried to snatch some sleep. I crawled under my jeep, but the flies pestered one unbearably. But this was almost preferable to a fitful doze with one's thoughts a turmoil of bearings and machine guns, jeep wheels and Messerschmitts, Stukas and burning vehicles. And the unending question, '*Will you operate on Fuka tonight? You must leave now*'.

So it was decided that this night we would drive back to the escarpment RV, and the following night set out for the rear of the enemy line. We would cover the lines with four parties, each one of two jeeps. The French in the central sector under their commander, Jordan, myself south of them, David Russell to the south of me, and a fourth patrol between Russell and the Qattara Depression. We would thus each cover a fifteen mile sector, and our job would be to destroy enemy soft-skinned vehicles, anything except armour. We hoped to find their leaguers lying about five miles behind their lines, where they would be collected for the night.

In our five nights away we had some hair-raising adventures, probing to within five miles behind the German front line at Alamein. I took Corporal Lambie, my tried and tested gunner, with me. This was our sixth successive operation together and he was as exhausted as I was, but we were alert enough to realize that no target we could find in the dark justified the loss of the whole patrol. Finally we were spotted and surrounded by tanks escaping only by the skin of our teeth.

Luck was with us and we found our way back to our old hideout.

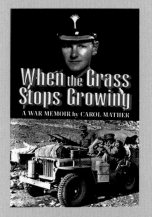

THE RAID ON CRETE

In April 1942, George Jellicoe, son of the former First Sea Lord during the Great War, reported to the do-it-yourself headquarters of Stirling's newly founded L5 Detachment, SAS Regiment at Kabrit. By April 1942 the detachment was very much in business carrying out raids on Axis airfields, roads and installations deep inside enemy territory. It was time to branch out.

By Lorna Almonds Windmill

Extracted from *A British Achilles* and reproduced by permission of Pen & Sword Books Ltd.

David Stirling gave Earl Jellicoe responsibility for liaison with the squadron of Free French parachutists who had joined the SAS at Kabrit. Their leader. Commandant Georges Bergé, was a tough, resilient character from Gascony. Jellicoe acted as their guide to British naval and military habits, counsellor and friend. His fluent French made him perfect for the assignment. Stirling, typically, was drawing fully on all available skills.

The Free French were a small unit but, as Jellicoe was to say years later, *'they were very, very free and very, very French'*. They had already served with distinction in South Africa, Palestine, Libya and Syria, before arriving

'From the outset, and showing his extraordinary foresight, Stirling was keen that the SAS be prepared to mount raids by sea.'

in Kabrit in January 1942, following an agreement between Stirling and Bergé that they should join forces. The Free French were all trained parachutists but needed to be fully integrated into the SAS. This task fell to Jellicoe and he designed joint fitness and endurance training for the French and British SAS men and special courses in demolition and weapon training.

The French were also greatly struck by the fact that, in contrast to themselves, Jellicoe was always smartly turned out in his 'so British' uniform, as they called it even when speaking French. It was a huge delight to them that Jellicoe operated in French. This removed many potential difficulties and helped bind the two nationalities together into one effective team.

ACTION

By May 1942, the trained and integrated men were badged and ready for action. This took the form of a daring raid on Heraklion airfield in the north of Crete. The mountainous island, 260 kilometres long, 103 kilometres wide and only 112 kilometres south-east of mainland Greece, had fallen to the Germans the year before as the German Army swept all before it throughout mainland Europe.

The aim of the raid was to reduce the strength of German air attacks on a supply convoy from Alexandria destined for Malta. The island was on the point of collapse and Churchill was adamant that vitally needed supplies should get through. The SAS raiders were to land by sea and blow up German bombers – particularly Junkers 88s – at Heraklion.

The assault, timed for the night of 12 June, was planned to coincide with SBS raids on other Cretan airfields at Maleme, Kastelli Pediados and Tymbaki. But it was typical of Stirling that he inserted himself into high-level operational planning and earmarked for the

George, 2nd Earl Jellicoe.

SAS the key target of Heraklion. For good measure, seven other German and Italian air bases in Cyrenaica were also to be attacked by the SAS, with all assaults coinciding with the passage of a Malta convoy. Operation *Vigorous*. On leaving Alexandria, it would face heavy enemy naval and aerial bombardment to the south-west of Crete.

In front of a large tent at Kabrit, which served as officers' mess, instruction room and meeting room, Bergé formed up his thirty men to hand pick those for the raid. The selection process was swift. '*Mouhot, Sibard, Leostic, stay with me,*' he barked. The rest he stood down. Bergé had chosen Sergeant Jacques Mouhot and Riflemen Parachutists Jack Sibard, originally a seaman in the French merchant navy, and Pierre Leostic, who was only seventeen.

In great secrecy *Triton*, a submarine of the Free Greek Navy under command of Captain Kontogiannis, took on board the five SAS operatives and their equipment. Lieutenant Costas Petrakis, a Cretan, of the Royal

'Very, very free and very, very French'. The Free French were highly trained and used to form an SAS squadron. The French SAS men wear their parachute insignia above their right breast pocket.

The main target of the SAS raid at Crete, the Junkers 88s, which were based at the Heraklion airstrip.

open to reduce pressure on the ears.

The SAS spent their time memorizing the mountainous and inhospitable Cretan terrain and mastering details like the password for local agents, 'I am Captain Manolis'.

A rendezvous had been arranged for their return at the village of Krotos on the south side of the island and at Gallos further to the west. After five days at sea, *Triton* surfaced off the north coast of Crete. Jellicoe's first sight of the island and of Greece was through the periscope of the submarine: a long dark mass seen only intermittently through the waterline lapping across the viewfinder. *Triton* dived again to about a dozen metres to await H hour.

In the early hours of 10 June, *Triton* dropped the SAS three miles out from the small beach at Karteros. This was much further than they had anticipated and they were faced with a long haul in with their paddles.

Hellenic Army, had joined the party and was to be their guide. Before embarking, the group carried out water training in inflatable dinghies. This preparation was important since the inflatables were frail and not very manoeuvrable. Jellicoe took one with Mouhot and Petrakis. Bergé, Sibard and Leostic took another from which they towed one with equipment, weapons and bombs. Each man carried a thirty kilo burden containing dry rations, water, explosives, detonators in separate oilskin bags and twenty-five plastic bombs. This weight was in addition to his weapons: a Colt 45, a Beretta machine gun, modified by Bergé to be more compact, an American dagger, two hand grenades, plastic bombs, compass, maps, aerial photographs and various small gadgets.

The submarine, *Triton*, had a fine Greek commander and an excellent crew. However, being a fairly basic French vessel built in the early 1920s, she was not very comfortable. The cramped conditions were exacerbated by the fact that the submarine was never meant for passengers. With several nationalities on board, differences of language and culture also had to be overcome. Despite these difficulties, Kontogiannis and his crew made the SAS very welcome, willingly engaging in three-way hot bunking so that each man could get about eight hours' sleep out of twenty-four. *Triton's* dives lasted for up to eighteen hours and life on board was strict. There could be no unnecessary noise and smoking was not allowed when the submarine dived. When they surfaced, before the hatch was opened, the officer of the watch advised everyone to rest with mouth

> 'Fifty or sixty Ju88 bombers were parked around the runways. Berge and Jellicoe then made a recce for a spot to get onto the airfield. It was the night of 13/14 June.'

Commando water training was beginning to pay off. As in training, Jellicoe, Petrakis and Mouhot were in one boat, towing one with the stores and explosives. Sibard and Leostic paddled another, with Bergé at the helm, which also towed a loaded boat. Then the dinghies began to leak. Jellicoe, always immaculate when going into action, immediately took off his gold-trimmed, peaked hat and started baling.

After some hours, the sound of waves breaking on a beach told the raiders that they had reached the small creek of San Barbara. There was no reception party so it was important to conceal all trace of their arrival. After unloading the inflatables and filling them with large stones, Jellicoe and Mouhot undressed, swam out with them several hundred yards from the shore and stabbed them, sending them gurgling to the bottom. The party was about twenty-five miles from their target and so left the beach, in single file, not even stopping to check for mines. They passed a shepherd who greeted them amiably with a 'Yassou', as if the sight of sinister SAS men on a Cretan beach at three o'clock in the morning was totally unremarkable.

By now, the operation was well behind schedule. It was impossible to reach a lying up point close to the airfield that night so they stopped to rest. Some friendly Cretan peasants, who never failed to spot anyone turning up like this, soon found them. Even the occupying Germans knew that the civilian population of Crete always gave all possible assistance to what later became known as 'the sabotage organization of Captain Jellicoe'.

The Bristol Beaufighter and nose camera photograph showing a rocket attack on an enemy target.

On the night of 12/13 June, the party moved off and got up close to the barbed wire surrounding the airfield. Then they almost ran into a German patrol. The situation was hopeless: they could have overcome the patrol but their cover would have been blown. So the attackers withdrew to the south-west to lie up through the day at a vantage point from which they could watch the airfield. Fifty or sixty Ju88 bombers were parked around the runways. Bergé and Jellicoe then made a recce for a spot to get onto the airfield. It was the night of 13/14 June.

While they were cutting their way through the barbed wire, another enemy patrol appeared. Jellicoe thought they had not been seen, but the last German in the column challenged them. With astonishing inspiration, Mouhot instantly rolled onto his back and began to snore loudly. The snores were so reverberatingly realistic and the Germans so clearly disgusted by the apparently drunken Cretan peasants that without more ado, they moved on. Mouhot's action saved the day because if the SAS had engaged the enemy, the raiding opportunity would have been lost. Thus the lack of curiosity and diligence of two German patrols gave the SAS their chance. The

Top right and below: The combined efforts of the SAS and the Royal Air Force caused large scale damage to German aircraft and equipment.

Germans were good soldiers but bad sentries.

Much encouraged, the raiders cut their way onto the airfield. Annoyingly, the German patrol returned. But then came a second piece of good luck: two Beaufighters attacked the airfield. This unexpected diversionary cover enabled the SAS to get to one of the two clumps of aircraft, where they set about placing bombs on twenty-two aircraft, including one Fieseler Fil56 Storch, a highly efficient, slow-flying reconnaissance aircraft, and some petrol dumps.

While Mouhot and Sibard were fixing their Lewes bombs to the wings of the aircraft (nineteen Ju88s, one

THE RAID ON CRETE

Me109, one Do17 and the Fieseler Storch), each with a two-hour time pencil fuse, Jellicoe with his *flegme britannique* (British cool) said to Bergé, in French, '*Commandant, I'm just going off to see if there is anything else to be done*'. Some time later, he reappeared, having planted more bombs on the engines of some still-crated aircraft and on several trucks.

The first bomb went off. The whole airfield was suddenly wide awake. The intruders now could not tackle any more aircraft, as they had planned. But how to get out of the airfield? A German patrol was marching out of the west gate and without any hesitation Bergé led the party forward. The SAS moved out, fell in smartly behind the patrol and at the appropriate moment outside the perimeter fence neatly peeled off into the darkness. They had not even been noticed. At that moment, there was a final explosion and a huge conflagration, the sound magnified by the closeness of the hills. The whole bomb depot had gone up. Bergé was delighted. They had done plenty of damage and Jellicoe immediately congratulated their leader. Hardly pausing to comment, Bergé responded, '*Mouhot, Sibard and Leostic – and you too Jellicoe – you're all going to get the Croix de Guerre. And Sibard you're promoted to corporal as from today.*' In addition to the aircraft, which included seventeen serviceable Ju88s, they had destroyed two aero engines, two trucks and the bomb dump.

It was still dark. The party quickly put as much distance as possible between themselves and the airfield, heading, as they thought, south with Bergé leading. Before long, Jellicoe drew Sibard's attention to the Pole Star in the sky up ahead of them. The Frenchman quickly understood that Bergé was leading them north. Since this would have been rather a disaster, Sibard casually queried with his Commandant whether they were in fact going in the right direction, whereupon Bergé, somewhat piqued, said, '*All right then, you take the lead if you're so clever*'. But instead, he called a halt to get their bearings while Petrakis went off to seek news. He returned a couple of hours later with a Cretan couple, a demobilized army officer and his wife, who brought a stew of courgettes and snails. The food went straight down. Some young Cretans appeared, curious to see what had happened. Though Jellicoe could not understand them, they intimated in no uncertain terms that he should leave as fast as he could. The Cretan had, after all, turned out to be that rarest of rare birds, a Cretan Quisling.

The French had indeed been betrayed. At about 1900 hours, as they had been preparing to move off, Berge had suddenly shouted, '*Look out! We're surrounded!*' The four men were trapped in a culvert with the mountain towering around them. They made a square and tried to take shelter behind a high bluff, with Bergé and Mouhot to the west and Sibard and Leostic facing 180 degrees to the east. A troop of Germans approached. They had clearly been well informed.

Bergé immediately opened fire and a German crumpled. Another German shouted orders as the enemy took cover among the scrub. There was a confusion of rifle fire and grenades. Bullets ricocheted off rocks and it was difficult for the Frenchmen to know where to aim. Then Leostic yelled, 'Let's go south! There's nobody there.' But Sibard had seen a German firing from that direction. 'No! Pierrot! No!' he screamed. But it was too late. Leostic had launched himself southwards and within a second there was a short burst of machine-gun fire. After a moment's silence, Sibard could hear his comrade moaning, 'Maman, Maman'. The German fired again. The crescendo of gunshots was followed by an even more awful silence. The young French soldier lay dead. He was just seventeen.

Being out of ammunition and hopelessly outnumbered, the French decided to surrender. At their shouts, the enemy held their fire. After a last attempt at evasion, the three Frenchmen were eventually captured. The Germans lost no time in interrogating their prisoners.

'There are six of you. Where are the others?' they demanded and, more menacingly, 'You General de Gaulle soldiers. You terrorists. You kaput.' Fortunately for the new POWs, it was the German air force at Heraklion, rather than the Gestapo, who interrogated them. The Luftwaffe did this thoroughly but engaged in no foul play or torture. On 2 July, the captives were flown out to Italy.

Meanwhile, Jellicoe had returned to the rendezvous. A few mornings later, walking along the beach, he was spotted in the binoculars of David Sutherland, who identified him by his khaki shorts and shirt and his jaunty walk. Sutherland's raid on Tymbaki had been aborted because the airfield was empty. The two men lay up for two nights in a cave where they suffered the most appalling fleabites.

23 June. John Campbell in HMS Porcupine arrived at night to pick up Jellicoe, Sutherland and the remaining SBS men to take them back to Mersa Matruh. As they were being ferried out to the ship, they passed an Englishman being brought to the island. It was Paddy Leigh Fermor, operating with the Special Operations Executive (SOE) out of Cairo, on his way in to begin a singularly successful partnership with the Cretan resistance. He and Jellicoe could not see each other but exchanged names by shouting.

'I'm Paddy Leigh Fermor. Who are you?' the new arrival bellowed across the wine-dark sea. 'George Jellicoe,' Jellicoe shouted back. 'Good luck!'

Leigh Fermor and his radio operator were the only men landing from Porcupine. As they went ashore, a crowd of guerrillas waited to be taken off but there was simply no room on the boat for them.

The SAS and SBS raids together had destroyed twenty-

The trawler HMS Porcupine, commanded by the SOE skipper John Campbell, which picked Jellicoe up after the raid on Crete.

six aircraft, fifteen to twenty trucks and considerable quantities of POL, bombs and other munitions. Despite this destruction, the convoy from Alexandria to Malta was forced to return to port after sustaining several losses. But ships from the convoy from Gibraltar got through. The attacks also contributed to the substantial overall harassment of the Axis forces.

'The earth came rushing up to meet me and I plunged into a small tree which cushioned my twenty feet per second fall. I released my harness and spent a frustrating time ripping the 'chute from the branches. As soon as I had got it clear I scraped a hole with my knife and buried it.'

THE SAS IN ITALY 1943

We were to be dropped into Northern Italy to derail trains in tunnels by explosives, the purpose being to reduce the flow of enemy troops and materials to the front. Captain Pinckney was a highly respected officer with an impressive record, a big man in every sense of the word, six foot plus yet never needing to raise his voice.

By Draper and Challenor

Extracted from *Tanky Challenor - SAS and the Met* and reproduced by permission of Pen & Sword Books Ltd.

Quietly, in a matter-of-fact tone, he outlined our various tasks particularly warning of the likelihood of encountering sentries guarding the tunnels. 'You'll know how to handle that problem' he said, and we all laughed. He made it sound like a picnic jaunt to Hampstead Heath, although we knew it would be anything but that. In a small outfit such as ours little remained secret for long, and it was soon common knowledge that Colonel Bill Stirling (David's brother) thought that not enough aircraft and men had been allocated for what he considered a vital operation. The whole Allied advance could be affected by the success or failure of our mission.

If his advice had been heeded, German reinforcements to the Salerno bridgehead by rail would have been negligible and lines of communication totally disrupted. We were split into two groups, one under Captain Pinckney, the other under Captain Dudgeon, and we would be landed in two separate night drops. I felt distinctly uneasy; I had only made three jumps and none of them had been at night. What's more, we would be deep behind the enemy's lines in hostile mountain country. A further danger was that we were going into an unprepared dropping zone, and no one had the vaguest idea of the conditions we were likely to encounter.

The purpose of the operation – the destruction of trains in tunnels buried deep in the Appennines – seemed a piece of cake compared to what was to follow. Somehow, by guess and by God, we had to make our way back to friendly lines. Today technological advances have removed most of the hazards which faced us. If the Op had been mounted in Vietnam or the Falkland Islands the raiders would have gone in and out by helicopter the same night, but more than forty years ago we were totally dependent on Shanks's Pony and a hard footslog through enemy-held territory towards the Allied armies which had landed at Reggio on the toe of Italy, three days before the launch of Speedwell. That was

'The purpose of the operation – the destruction of trains in tunnels buried deep in the Appennines – seemed a piece of cake compared to what was to follow.'

some five hundred miles away, the distance from London to Aberdeen. It was optimistically estimated that the Allies would be advancing so quickly that contact would be made in a week. In wartime things seldom go according to plan, and that was certainly true of Speedwell.

Although the Italians surrendered on 8 September, the Germans reacted swiftly and skilfully, almost as if they were glad to be shot of the Eyties. They made full use of the inhospitable terrain which was more helpful to the defenders than the attackers, and the well-organized resistance kept the Allied advance to a snail's pace. That made the success of our operation much more imperative. By cutting the jugular vein of supplies, the Americans and British would be able to regain their momentum. Captain Pinckney and his seven-man group were to attack the Bologna-Florence and Borretta-Pistoia railway lines while Captain Dudgeon's group of six men, of which I was a member, was to be split into three parties. Captain Dudgeon and parachutists Brunt, Sergeant Foster and Corporal Shortall were to attack sections of the line between Genoa and La Spezia, while Lieutenant Wedderburn and I were assigned the line between La Spezia and Bologna.

Captain Dudgeon was only 23 but a splendid commander. He stood over six feet tall and was viewed as something of a Captain Bligh character. Oddly enough it did not diminish the affection we held him. He was a strict disciplinarian who could raise a laugh where other men would have brought scowls of discontent. Charisma was not a word that was in common use then, but it certainly applied to him. At Philippeville, while orderly officer, he strode into the marquee where lunch was being served. A special treat on the menu that day was lemonade. He marched up to the first table and put the time-honoured question: '*Any complaints?*' '*Yes, sir,*' ventured a bold voice, '*Not much powder in the lemonade, sir.*' He rapped his swagger stick on the table like someone quelling a mutinous rabble. '*Give the men WATER.*' We all responded with a rousing cheer. Captain Dudgeon, out of earshot, was somewhat incongruously called Toomai, after the elephant boy in one of Kipling's stories, though he was, in fact, built on the massive scale of the elephant itself and would charge through the thickest undergrowth.

After the initial briefing, the next forty-eight hours sped by in a whirlwind of activity which left us with little time to brood on what lay ahead. We checked and re-checked maps and all the other paraphernalia of an

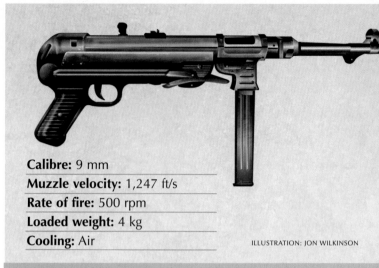

Calibre: 9 mm
Muzzle velocity: 1,247 ft/s
Rate of fire: 500 rpm
Loaded weight: 4 kg
Cooling: Air

ILLUSTRATION: JON WILKINSON

MP 40 SUBMACHINE GUN

operation, loaded the tube-like panniers with ammunition, explosives and foodstuffs, and cleaned and re-cleaned our weapons. I was armed with a first-class and most lethal Schmeisser machine pistol, drawn from the SAS armoury of captured weapons. It had a 9 mm calibre 32-cartridge magazine and was capable of firing five hundred rounds per minute effectively up to a range of 150 yards.

Over our uniforms we wore US blue-grey overalls which at a distance made us resemble Germans. I also carried a .32 pistol, and strapped to my leg was a combat knife honed to a razor sharpness for close-quarter work on sentries. Apart from them we had been told not to attack any other troops if it could be avoided. We were to be as silent and as secretive as possible; the destruction of vital supplies was our main object. If any explosives were left after we had completed our line blowing, it was to be used in nuisance attacks on electric pylons and telephone lines.

Our food was very basic: bully beef and sardines, raisins and cheese, plenty of char and tins of fifty Players cigarettes. Each man was also issued with thousands of lira with which to pay Italian peasants who might help us with food and shelter, and every officer was given several gold coins, worth about £10 each, as a reserve currency to be used only as a last resort. It was the only time I had found the army to be generous with money.

A cloak and dagger touch was added to the operation by our Intelligence Officer, Major Eric Barkworth. His inventive mind produced a stream of intriguing emergency devices. Being a pipe smoker, I was issued with a pipe with a minute compass secreted in the stem, and inside the lining of the pouch was a silk map of Italy.

Tanky Challenor.

The Armstrong Whitworth Albemarle, the aircraft used to drop SAS operators behind enemy lines.

In view of what was to happen to me I would have preferred an extra change of boots and underwear.

Although we were dropping into an unknown future, we were afforded no special privileges on the morning of D-Day. Reveille was at 7.30 am and we had our usual breakfast. There was no marked tension, just an air of general excitement and anticipation. We were impatient to get cracking.

In the afternoon we had a final briefing at which Captain Dudgeon warned us that if we were forced to drop from a height we should be careful to check our drift so that on landing we could link up with the others. Shop talk over, he produced a bottle of whisky which we drank among the olive trees. At 5.00 pm we boarded a truck and drove out to the Albemarle standing on the edge of the air strip where mechanics crawled ant-like over the wings and engines making a final check. Normally I experienced a tightening of the stomach which was invariably a sign of trouble ahead, but I felt nothing. I was completely at ease, just as if I was embarking on a training exercise.

The engines fired into life and we taxied along the dusty runway before lifting off like an overfed pelican straining to become airborne. Ahead lay an uncomfortable 5¹/₂-hour flight before we reached our objective in Northern Italy – the high ground near Bergo val di Taro, north of La Spezia.

The Albemarle, which carried a crew of two pilots, radio operator and navigator, was only equipped to take ten paratroopers, so we were very cramped indeed in the space forward of the large dropping hole in the floor at the rear of the fuselage. It meant we had little leg room, and if we wanted to ease our cramp-stiffened limbs we had to be careful not to bang our heads.

Soon after crossing the coast we were in complete darkness, unable to read or smoke in the blacked-out plane, and there was little to do but lean back on our parachute packs and doze or talk. I couldn't snooze so I joined in the aimless chatter and we talked without any real knowledge or conviction about the respective merits of Italian women and Arab women, and whether the

booze where we were going would be an improvement.

There was no heating in the Albemarle but we were packed in so close to each other that we became hot and sticky under our denims, and the urge to add to the smog by smoking became almost unbearable. Shortly before midnight the pilot passed word that we were crossing the Italian coast. We would never have guessed it, but for a short burst of flak which ceased abruptly as we flew inland. *'Ten minutes to go!'* warned the Despatcher, opening the hatch in the fuselage floor. Immediately the slipstream roared in, chilling the sweat on our bodies. We rose unsteadily and began to go through the familiar stages preceding a drop. We got into jumping order; checked our equipment by the shaded light which had been switched on and glowed like a bloodshot eye, made sure our static lines were correctly attached to the strong points, and examined the ties on each others' 'chutes. We were now ready for the Despatcher's orders.

Captain Dudgeon had almost to shout to make himself heard above the inrush of air and the roar of the engines.

'Remember to watch your drift going down. The stick is to stay as tight as possible. I will

The point of no return. A Paratroop stick descending to a target area.

41

remain where I land and you are to walk to me, number six walking on to number five and so on, until we pick each other up.'

The light flashed. *'Number one,'* yelled the Despatcher, slapping Captain Dudgeon on the shoulder. He disappeared out of the hole and we followed in quick succession. We knew there was no danger of being too close in a multi-paratroop drop. As soon as you leave the aircraft the slipstream whisks you away, but if there is too long an interval between jumps the stick becomes spread out and separated by ever-increasing gaps, which get even bigger on landing.

I was Number six in the dropping order and therefore last out. I remember gasping for air as the icy slipstream caught me. This was followed by the stomach-wrenching feeling of falling free. Then there was a hard jerk on my shoulders as the canopy billowed open above me I looked up to make sure my rigging lines were not twisted, and I saw the Albemarle disappear to the right. Then I checked the position of the rest of the stick; they were dead ahead, swinging gently in a straight line and strung out in perfect formation about 100 yards from each other. We could have conducted a conversation in the still night air; in that rarified atmosphere sound is magnified and travels quickly.

To the left, in the direction of La Spezia, an air raid siren wailed mournfully. *'A bit bloody late with the alarm clock,'* I said to myself.

It was a perfect night, cloudless and moonlit, and down below the Appennines looked like gentle hillocks. It had been a high drop, 7,000 feet, the highest I had ever made. My three previous ones had been in the region of 300 feet, aimed at hitting the deck as quickly as possible. This time we were in no great hurry.

The earth came rushing up to meet me and I plunged into a small tree which cushioned my twenty feet per second fall. I released my harness and spent a frustrating time ripping the 'chute from the branches. As soon as I had got it clear I scraped a hole with my knife and buried it. I looked around and saw I had landed in a small copse on a scrub-filled mountainside. I began to walk on my line bearing to link up with Lieutenant Wedderburn, using a low whistling sound which was our pre-arranged recognition signal. An hour later I had linked up with him.

Captain Dudgeon had a rapid roll call and was gratified to learn that there had been no injuries or hitches; it had gone as smoothly as a practice run. He then satisfied himself that no immediate alarm had been sounded and that our location was far enough from any large mountain track for us to be able to relax for a few hours before searching for the supply

'Our partings were low key, in typical unemotional SAS style, just a cheery wave and a call of 'Good luck'.

containers at first light. A sentry was posted and we stretched out on the ground and lit our first cigarettes since leaving base. Our wads were char-less: the tea was in the containers with the rest of the provisions and our sleeping bags. But it was a warm night and we could happily do without either.

At dawn we were awakened by birds and the impressive spectacle of a red sun climbing up over the rim of the Appennines. I shinned up a tree and located the containers through my binoculars. The distinctive red and blue 'chutes were directly ahead and only 200 yards away. They stood out like a sixpence on a sweep's backside, and we hastened towards them before anyone else spotted them. Everything was intact and when we carried them to the scene of our bivouac Captain Dudgeon gave us the go-ahead to light a fire. We opened tins of bully and brewed up tea, the first drink and food we had had for several hours. For the rest of the day we did little but check and re-check our bearings on salient landmarks, climbing trees to confirm our position, and poring over maps. Then we worked out our compass bearings, for the next move at nightfall – the route to our individual targets. Then we buried the containers and waited for dusk.

A rendezvous was arranged for seven nights ahead, at a point on a stream between Pontremoli and Villafranca. Our partings were low key, in typical unemotional SAS style, just a cheery wave and a call of *'Good luck'*. The other four marched off in single file along a wooded mountain track. That was the last I saw of them. Later we heard of their fate. Captain Dudgeon and parachutist Brunt ambushed a German truck and killed the occupants, then used the vehicle to make faster progress towards their objective, but after a short time they were captured at an enemy road block. The following morning, without a trial, they were executed by firing squad. A German doctor who was present wrote to Captain Dudgeon's father at the end of the war and said they both died bravely and with

A German firing squad in progress. This was a fate that awaited SAS soldiers if captured behind the lines.

dignity. Their graves were located after war and they were reburied in the military cemetery in Florence.

Sergeant Foster and Corporal Shorthall were never seen or heard of again, and to this day nothing is known of their fate.

Left alone on the side of a mountain, Lieutenant Wedderburn and I checked our compass bearings once more, then set off towards our own objective.

As I looked at the stocky figure of Lieutenant Wedderburn trudging ahead of me, back bent under the weight of his pack, legs thrusting him forward like a skilled climber, I reflected that only in an SAS unit on a hush-hush behind-the-lines job could two such contrasting men have been tossed together. In peacetime we would never have met, having little in common and coming from such different social backgrounds.

We were chalk and cheese in nearly every respect. I was strongly built, deep chested, over 5 feet 10 inches tall and from a not-too-happy working-class home where, from my elementary school, I had been tossed into the deep end of life to make my own way from one dead-end job to another. I was stubborn, defiant, a trifle wild, but totally loyal to anyone who commanded my respect.

Thomas MacLeggan Wedderburn, on the other hand, was an upper-middle-class Scot from Edinburgh whose law studies had been interrupted by the war. Pushing thirty, he was fairly old for an SAS officer, but he was tremendously strong and his mountaineering experience, gained from peacetime climbing in the Highlands and the Swiss Alps, made him an indispensable member of the Speed-well team. He was stockily built and on the short side; the top of his head was on a level with my chest, and he peered owlishly through thick heavy-framed glasses. It was inevitable that he was nicknamed 'Tojo'. So there we were, Tojo and Tanky, out looking for a railway tunnel in which to create trouble.

We climbed steadily through the night up steep slopes studded with rocks and scrub stopping every now and then for Lieutenant Wedderburn to make compass checks. Although it was a clear moonlit night, taking accurate bearings was difficult and our progress was slow.

SAS AND SRS RAIDS IN ITALY 1943-44

'We slogged on night after night, sleeping as best we could during the day under any bush that offered reasonable concealment. We were seven days into our mission before we found a tunnel.'

It was 3.00 am and visibility had considerably improved when we nudged each other and pointed to the bottom of a mountain opposite; snaking around the foot was a railway line with a bridge spanning a wide stream. We cautiously clambered down, careful not to dislodge any loose stones, to examine the bridge, but after close scrutiny agreed that we would have needed a truckload of explosives to blow such a massive structure. Slightly disappointed, we consoled ourselves by reminding each other that our objective was to blow trains in tunnels, and so we decided to follow the lines throughout the remainder of the day in the hope of coming across a tunnel.

We slogged on night after night, sleeping as best we could during the day under any bush that offered reasonable concealment. We were seven days into our mission before we found a tunnel. The lines disappeared into a mountain, and we were in no doubt that it had to be a long one, a comforting thought because it meant we

British Special Forces undergoing railway sabotage training.

could lay charges a considerable distance from each other on the 'Up' and 'Down' lines. Once placed in position we would have plenty of time to leg it to safety.

We kept observation from a nearby vantage point and noticed that there seemed to be lengthy intervals between trains entering and emerging from the tunnel, and that most of the traffic consisted of goods trains.

We checked our charges and transferred them to smaller packs. To blow a line we would need 3 lbs of plastic 808, which looked as harmless as sticks of plasticine. The sticks would be taped to the rails and connected by instantaneous cortex fuse to an ordinary fog signal detonator inserted into a gun cotton primer. It was crude but effective. When the wheels ran over the fog signal it detonated the whole lot and blew out a section of the line. The train was derailed and as the trucks ploughed into each other the tunnel would be completely blocked from roof to floor. Clearing it would be a long and laborious task. At least, that was the theory. In practice we had yet to see it work. Just before midnight we crept down to the mouth of the tunnel leaving our larger packs behind in our hide-out. It was dark and the moon had deserted the sky, so Lieutenant Wedderburn had the bright idea of attaching strips of the tape, used for binding up the explosives, on the occasional rock or bush to assist us in making our getaway.

We assumed that the tunnel would have sentries posted – it was after all a vital supply line – so I slipped ahead with my knife at the ready to pierce from behind the heart of any sentry. I volunteered for the job as I considered myself something of a dab hand as a silent killer. To reach the entrance I had to splash through a small stream running alongside the line. The gurgling and splashing of the water over stones helped to deaden any sound I made; even so I paused every few seconds to listen for a challenge from the mouth of the tunnel,

but none came. I took no chances because sentries are renowned for slipping off to have a quick drag at a cigarette, but after a stealthy inspection I realised one had not been posted. I felt quite deflated and I thought, *'Easy drop, now no bloody sentries.'* I returned to Lieutenant Wedderburn and whispered, *'All clear. Now let's go and get a train or two.'*

Inside the tunnel it was as dark as a cellar and as cold as charity, and we stumbled along like blind men, tapping on the line which was a substitute for a white stick. Gradually our eyes became adjusted to the dark and 100 yards into the tunnel we attached our first charges on the outside rail of the 'Down' line from Pontremoli, a job which took only five minutes but seemed like years.

We stumbled on for a considerable distance and planted more charges on the 'Up' line. Despite the chilling cold, we were both sweating and I needed no urging when Lieutenant Wedderburn whispered, *'Well done, Tanky. Let's get out of here.'*

We were walking out as fast as the conditions would allow when suddenly I heard it. I straightened up, craned my head, and said,

'Listen! There's a bloody train coming.'

We stood immobile in the darkness as 'Tojo' listened intently. There was no doubt about it, a train was approaching fast, making the line hum. And it was travelling on the 'Down' line where we had placed the

Silent killing. This was an essential part of Special Forces training, a necessary evil for neutralising enemy sentries guarding key targets.

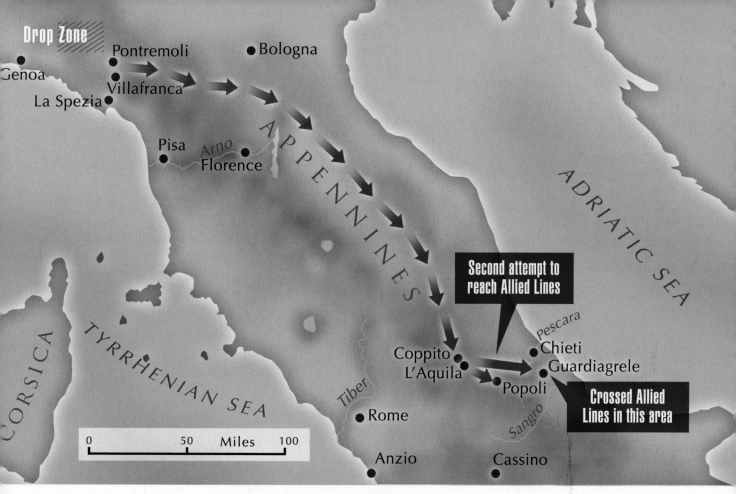

CHALLENOR'S ESCAPE ROUTE TO ALLIED LINES

first set of charges. '*Good God*' said Wedderburn. '*Move man. Run like hell.*'

I needed no prompting. I ran like an Olympic sprinter with 'Tojo' prepared to settle for Silver. Neither of us had any wish to be buried at the scene of our triumph. The train seemed to be getting closer as we headed for the small circle of light ahead. Our boots caught against the line and sleepers, and our lungs were near to bursting, sheer desperation propelling us at a speed we would never again match.

As we broke clear of the entrance we hurled ourselves into the stream just in time to see the train thundering into the tunnel. Seconds later there was a rumbling boom magnified by the confined space of the tunnel. This was followed by the screeching and rending of metal being torn apart and piling up against the roof. Dense smoke billowed out of the cavernous entrance. We stuck up our thumbs in a gesture of triumph – without doubt the train had been well and truly derailed.

We clambered out of the stream wringing wet but smiling. Then we heard the rumble of a train on the 'Up'

Tanky in 1945 after being awarded the MM for his exploits behind the German lines.

line. We listened in awe for the inevitable boom. When it came it was even louder than the first. Again it was followed by the awful rending of steel and splintering of wood. Then an eerie silence descended.

The two Ts – Tanky and Tojo – had claimed two trains at one go and completely blocked the La Spezia-Bologna line as ordered.

We soon found the first of the tape markers, and followed the trail that led us back to our big packs, and, without pausing to take a look at the devastation we had wreaked, we headed up into the mountains, anxious to put as much distance as possible between us and our handiwork. Within minutes the place would be crawling with Germans.

ESCAPE AND EVASION

After blowing up two trains, Tanky was captured, beaten and tortured by the SS. He managed to escape his captors and walked 300 miles before being captured again. He escaped yet again and managed to successfully break through the German Gustav line and dash across No Man's Land into the safety of British positions.

'When the parties rallied it was discovered that Lieutenants Poole and Fowles were missing. The four troopers buried their parachutes and, as the visibility was good, carried out a prolonged and widespread search for the containers.'

DIGITAL RECONSTRUCTION: JON WILKINSON

SAS IN EUROPE – OVERLORD 1944

Operation *Titanic* IV was the first operation carried out by SAS troops in north-west Europe. Six men and one aircraft were involved, and although *Titanic* IV is mentioned in several books about the Regiment it is usually dismissed as only a small part of a deception ploy, implying that it was almost an irrelevancy. Closer scrutiny confirms that it was indeed a tiny part of a huge plan encompassing, but not restricted to, Operations *Fortitude North* and *South*, without which the invasion of Normandy would not have been successful.

By Francis Mackay

Extracted from *Overture to Overlord* and reproduced by permission of Pen & Sword Books Ltd.

Operation *Titanic* was the overall code-name allocated to simulated paratroop landings behind the German coastal defence zone, intended to disperse German anti-paratroop forces (usually battalions of light infantry mounted on bicycles) and to draw attention away from real landings in Normandy. *Titanic* was part of Operation *Taxable*, itself a small but vital part of Operation *Fortitude South*, the deception plan for *Overlord*.

The original *Taxable* plan included several simulated paratroop landings, of which Operations *Titanic* I–IV are the best known. Only IV was mounted due to lack of transport aircraft, and scarcity of SAS troops due to the delays in getting 1 and 2 SAS back to Britain.

Titanic I was to simulate an airborne division landing on a DZ north of the River Seine, in an upland area called the Pays du Caux, south of St Valery. The aim was to lure enemy reserves, especially the formidable *12 SS Panzer-Division Hitler Jugend*, north of the river and away from the invasion beaches and the few (deliberately) undamaged bridges over the river, leading to the Juno and Gold assault areas. A subsidiary aim was to reinforce the Germans' fixation that the invasion would be in the Pas de Calais, further reinforced by deception operations off the coast between Le Havre and Dieppe, simulating an invasion fleet heading for the Pas de Calais. One involved motor launches towing barrage-balloons ends of roads running on embankments crossing low-lying ground behind the Utah assault areas; ground that had been inundated by the Germans as a defence measure.

The JPS regarded the role of these airborne divisions as critical to the successful exploitation of the Utah landings. The second airborne wave would include gliders carrying bulldozers to enlarge the exits from the roads and to make gun positions, and anti-tank guns to repel the expected counter-attacks by *Panzers* and *Panzer-Grenadiers* in half-tracks.

Therefore anything which might ensure the success of the American operations was to be welcomed. Their secondary mission was to protect the southern flank of US VII Corps landing on Utah, and also to be prepared to exploit southward through Carentan. The latter task was to be carried out by destroying two bridges on the main Carentan highway and the railroad bridge west of it, by seizing and holding the la Barquette lock, and finally by establishing a bridgehead over the River Douve north-east of Carentan.

The SAS were up against a formidable enemy, the 12 SS Panzer-Division. Their task was to keep these troops busy whilst the invasion was in progress.

Paratroopers of the 101st Airborne prepare to board a DC-3 on D-Day.

peninsula and had its headquarters in Périers, north of Coutances. Further south was the elusive *91 Luftlande-Division*, and to the east was *354 Infanterie-Division*, which had a counter-attack role against sea or airborne landings along the coastal area of Normandy. It was based east of St Lô, with its headquarters in the small country town of Canisy. The fourth formation, Schnelle Brigade 30, was based to the south-west of St Lô, with headquarters in Cerences, south-west of Coutances. The brigade had at least one mobile unit trained in quick-reaction anti-airborne operations, mounted on bicycles; a primitive mode of transport but sufficient for patrolling roads and country lanes quickly and silently. The SAS Brigade Operational Instruction section on enemy dispositions then went on to state that:

'... all that is certain is that on D-Day the towns in the area will be full of troops at a high state of readiness; some of these troops may be on their way to the beaches. A vigorous response to Titanic *IV is probable; formed units could easily be on the DZ within one and a half hours and motor-cycle or cavalry patrols should be reconnoitring within half an hour of landing.'*

On 27 May the bulk of the SAS Brigade moved from Ayrshire to holding camps near airfields in the Cotswolds. The troops arrived late on 27 May and those detailed for operations between D-Day and D+14 moved from Cirencester station to a holding area, a transit camp near RAF Fairford. The camp held a large number

Three men of 1 SAS, one in French-style disguise, operating behind the lines.

The 101st was to be reinforced by its glider-borne infantry and artillery units landing at dusk on D-Day. The 82nd Airborne was to protect the approaches to Utah from the German *91 Luftlande Division*. On 25 May it was reported by SIS or the Resistance as harboured north of Saint Saveur le Vicomte. The German forces in Normandy were certainly weak, but one of their generals said later that although badly equipped, *'... his best weapons were his young NCOs, battle-hardened in Russia'*.

SAS TASKING

The *Titanic* IV mission was allocated to the SAS Brigade because, although it was to be in direct support of the 82nd and 101st Airborne divisions and into the American sector of the invasion area, there were no US troops available; no 6 SAS, for example. (The 7-man USMC OG would have been ideal.) The task was allocated to 1 SAS; some accounts state the task was 'offered' to Paddy Mayne by a junior staff officer, and that it was rejected on the grounds that it was an 'intelligence' operation, then 'offered' to, and accepted by, Lieutenant Colonel Franks, 2 SAS. No evidence has been found to support these contentions. The live element of Operation *Titanic* IV was conducted by troops from 1 SAS; three men from A Squadron, Lieutenant Frederick James Poole, Troopers Dawson and Saunders, and three from B Squadron, Lieutenant Norman Harry Fowles and Troopers Hurst and Merryweather. They faced considerable opposition. Enemy forces in the south Cotentin reportedly included four major formations. *243 Infanterie-Division* was tasked with the static defence of the west coast of the

of men as the teams for Operations *Titanic* IV, *Bulbasket*, *Houndsworth*, *Dingson*, *Samwest* and *Gain* were incarcerated there, along with the brigade command and administrative staff; nearly 500 men.

DEPARTURE

On 5 June Paddy Mayne travelled to Hassell Hall for a final word with his men. It is not clear whether the four troopers were allowed to eat and socialize with the officers; even if the regiment was considered egalitarian by the standards of the time they were probably more comfortable apart.

The Hall was busy with SOE agents, their conducting officers and staff officers from SOE as well as the SAS officers. The SAS officers spent much of the day with jigsaws, watching a film and chatting with two young women who helped them with the puzzles. The SAS troops obviously did not know who the two women were; Paul McCue in his book *Operation Bulbasket* reveals that one was Violette Szabo, about to depart on her second and last mission to France. She was captured by the Germans, interrogated and sent to Ravensbrück concentration camp where she was executed in 1945. Also close by were the three members of Jedburgh Team Hugh who were to fly with the *Bulbasket* reconnaissance team. Just before 2000 hours the *Titanic* and *Bulbasket* teams collected their Bergen rucksacks, radio and weapons and travelled by car to the airfield to collect their parachutes and pigeons.

The eighth Halifax, NF-M, flown by Flight Lieutenant Johnson, carried the *Titanic* IV teams and containers. It took off 'on time', and was logged back into Tempsford at 0300 hours on 6 June; the log entry simply states 'Dropped Party'; the RAF had played its part, and delivered the SAS teams to the DZ. The troops had jumped but it was not as simple as the log indicates.

The Halifax made an accurate landfall near Avranches and commenced the run-in to the DZ, and when the aircraft was estimated to be eight minutes away the navigator appears to

Paratrooper with messenger pigeon.

RAF pigeon parachute system.

have switched on the dispatcher's red standby light. But for some reason, stated as a malfunction in the lights, it changed to green, Go, almost immediately. When that happens there is no time to think; dispatcher and paratroops are staring at the light, mesmerized. When it changes the dispatcher screams 'Go', and they go – fast.

Violette Szabo, an SOE operative who was dropped behind the lines during 1944.

The result of the malfunctioning light was that the two teams were dropped about seven minutes ahead of schedule, at 0020 hours. They may have been momentarily flummoxed by the malfunctioning lights, and there appears to have been a slight pause before No. 2 in the stick followed Lieutenant Fowles through the Joe-hole; just a few seconds, enough to scatter the first man from the others. And to make matters worse, the last man, Lieutenant Poole, tripped over his leg-bag and 'rang the bell', knocking himself out in the process. (He must have been last as no one reported seeing him stumble.) The majority landed some two kilometres north-west of the intended DZ.

No report of dropping containers or the sight of Very lights or the sound of

The Halifax bomber: a taxi for the SAS and equipment.

simulated rifle fire have been located. When the parties rallied it was discovered that Lieutenants Poole and Fowles were missing. The four troopers buried their parachutes and, as the visibility was good, carried out a prolonged and widespread search for the containers. None were located, nor was there any sign of the two subalterns. The four troopers were on their own. As it was now 0300 hours, and there was a glimmer of light in the east, they decided to follow as best they could the instruction issued at Fairford. They spread out around the DZ and planted their Lewes bombs and withdrew. The bombs exploded, but failed to attract any immediate attention. The party moved to the north away from the landing area and hid in a thick hedge. They stayed there all day and saw no movement apart from a patrol of German bicycle troops on the St Lô-Carentan road. That evening, at about 2000 hours, they were contacted by a member of the local Resistance, named as Monsieur Edouard le Duc. How he located them is not known, unless they were spotted by a farmer or farm worker in or near the hedge. Monsieur le Duc advised the team – in what language they communicated is not known – that he would lead them away from the area later that night. He departed, but returned after about three hours, and led them westwards for about two miles to the ruins of an old abbey, possibly the Maison de Marais, next to the present day D 900, between St Lô and Périers. Monsieur le Duc helped the troopers find a hiding place, and then departed. The party remained hidden throughout D-Day, undisturbed and content to be safe; sounds of battle would have been faintly heard from the east. Monsieur le Duc returned

German soldiers inspecting the twisted wreckage of a train, sabotaged by enemy activity.

American troops advancing through the rubble of a street west of St Lô.

early the following morning, at around 0100 hours, bringing some food and cider but leaving soon afterwards. Later that morning the troopers' spirits rose considerably when Monsieur le Duc returned with Lieutenant Poole. He looked somewhat battered, and after the Frenchman departed explained what had happened since leaving the aircraft.

Apparently when the jump light changed from red to green and the dispatcher yelled, or screamed as most do, he, Poole, in his haste to leave the aircraft had stumbled and 'rang the bell' on the far side of the Joe-hole. The next thing he remembered was coming-to on the ground, still in his parachute harness. He checked his watch and realized he had been unconscious for about forty-five minutes. He managed to disentangle himself and buried the parachute. He also wrote a brief note explaining the circumstances of his arrival, and that there was no sign of the other troops. The message was dispatched by his pigeon, which had patiently endured the exit, uncontrolled descent and long wait before its temporary owner came to his senses. At some stage he appears to have lost the MCR-1, and there is no record of how, or where, he disposed of his Lewes bombs. At some time on D-Day he appears to have made contact with a farmer who hid him and advised Monsieur le Duc.

There was a concerted effort by all circuits to cut telephone and telegraph communications between Cherbourg, the Channel Islands and the rest of France. Particular attention was paid to cutting underground cables around Périers, and to keeping them cut. This little town was a communications hub through which ran many lines linking headquarters and defence sites. The cables had been located and sabotage sites selected during the previous year; at one time there was a large file of reports and maps plotting German and Milice power and telecommunications links in France, based on Resistance surveys.

The railways were strongly guarded as a group of enthusiastic 'unregistered', or freelance resisters, had sabotaged the Cherbourg turntable shortly before the landings, and the Germans had doubled the guards at key points, and reinforced their roving patrols. On 10 June Monsieur le Duc once again appeared at the abbey, and once more with a pleasant surprise – Lieutenant Fowles. The Frenchman departed soon afterwards, and the rest of the troops were able to recount their experiences since leaving the aircraft. Apparently Lieutenant Fowles had landed one field away from the DZ and had spent a considerable time searching for the others and the containers. He hid for a few days, occasionally sniping at some German soldiers but without apparent success. He also cut a few telephone wires strung along the side of a road leading to a German headquarters, again without being hunted. At some time in the afternoon, without volunteering an explanation to his colleagues, Lieutenant Fowles left the abbey but returned again at 2300 hours.

That night the group held a discussion and it was decided to stay in the abbey until overrun by the Allies, in accordance with the order issued in England. Their rations would have been running low by that time, but the food from the Resistance would have helped. Nothing much seems to have happened for the next two weeks.

On 25 June, well past the date the Allies were supposed to arrive, Monsieur le Duc appeared with three US paratroops; escaped prisoners of war. They were all from the 508th Parachute Infantry Regiment, 82nd Airborne Division. They were Captain Berry, a medical officer, and two unidentified privates, one wounded. All three had been dropped near Edenville on the night of 5–6 June, but well away from their DZs.

The Americans had little in the way of food so the supply situation became serious. It was resolved, in part, by foraging for vegetables but these could not be cooked as lighting a fire was out of the question and the supply of Hexamine tablets for the SAS men's cookers had long since been exhausted. On 28 June there was a very unwelcome break in the monotony when paratroops of *Fallschirmjäger-Regiment 6* took possession of a nearby village, Remilly-sur-Lozon. Monsieur le Duc had maintained contact with SAS troops after delivering the US paratroops to the hiding place and, when confirming the presence of the Germans, added that they knew there were Allied paratroops in the vicinity, and that the party should therefore move away from the area as soon as possible. That night he took them about three kilometres south, back to the vicinity of the original DZ. They remained hidden until the following night, when he returned and led them further south, for about two kilometres, to another hiding place, described as an old brushwood cabin where they hid for three days and nights. The wounded private seems to have been able to keep up with his companions, and his wound is not mentioned.

Fallschirmjäger *paratroopers were fighting as infantry men on D-Day to push back the Allied invaders.*

On the night of 8–9 July the party moved north again and arrived near the village of Raids, on the main road between Carentan and Périers. They went to earth about 400 metres from a German position being mortared by Allied troops. According to Trooper Hurst the party had many near misses from overshoots, but felt moving would be too dangerous. The following morning it was decided to recce the area ready for a break across no man's land that night, 9–10 July. The party were not well concealed, and unlucky. At about noon they spotted two German soldiers, reported as 'paratroops', advancing towards their position. The Germans spotted them, and threw several grenades before making off. The grenades exploded among the party. Captain Berry, Lieutenant Fowles and the uninjured private were slightly wounded, but Hurst was seriously injured in both legs, and Merryweather in the back. Neither could raise themselves far off the ground, let alone walk. The uninjured members of the party, Lieutenant Poole and Troopers Dawson and Saunders, carried Hurst and Merryweather to a nearby farm, helped by the three Americans. Lieutenant Fowles left the group, apparently intent on finding and silencing the Germans. The farm was about 150 metres from the scene of the incident, and only 700 metres from the nearest friendly forces, US troops advancing down the Cotentin peninsula towards Coutances. In the farm Captain Berry did what he could for his colleagues. They did not have much time to ponder their fate or decide what to do next, as their presence in the farm was, to quote Trooper Hurst, '... *revealed by the French',* possibly the farmer and his family leaving the premises in a hurry to avoid getting caught in a battle. The Germans must have interrogated the French, because they did not mount an attack on the farm, merely surrounded it as if aware the occupants were wounded. The cordon was formed by about forty

German paratroops dressed in camouflage suits and heavily armed with automatic weapons. Hurst later described them as being very young, white-faced and nervous. The senior German, a sergeant, shouted to the party to come out. The party had no option but to comply. They left the farm building carrying or supporting the wounded members, and were lined up, or laid down, in a row. They were lightly searched for weapons which were carefully removed and placed out of reach. The escape equipment carried by the SAS troops sewn into various places in their uniforms was not found.

PRISONERS OF WAR

The Germans escorted the party to a nearby position, a line of trenches along the north edge of a sunken lane, some of the Germans helping to carry the wounded SAS troopers. The party was escorted past the defence line and into an orchard and over to a hut that the Germans were using as a headquarters. Each man was briefly interrogated by one of the German officers, thought to have been a captain. The only questions asked of the troops were their number, rank and name. No other information was sought; the Germans probably realized their prisoners had no information of any tactical use in the current engagement. After two hours the party were moved to an advanced dressing station where a German Army medical officer attended to their wounds. They were also given some evil-tasting cigarettes, and some sweets and confectionery. The wounded were, by now, feeling the cumulative effects of the tension of the last few weeks in enemy territory, lack of hot food, or even any reasonable food, full of straw and 'pretty filthy' according to Hurst. Some of the Allied wounded were operated on by the German surgical team, who also had about fifty of their own to look after. Here Lieutenant Fowles reappeared. He was badly wounded in the back, and was carried into the monastery by a German soldier, and attended to by the German medical staff. At some point the three unwounded SAS troops, Poole, Dawson and Saunders, were taken away. They had a chance of a few words with Hurst before leaving, as he was just about to be taken into the operating 'theatre'. A couple of days later, on 13 July, he was taken by road to a temporary military hospital in Rennes, a long, uncomfortable and dangerous journey in a *Wehrmacht* lorry; one of a convoy of twenty vehicles filled with wounded soldiers, enemy and Allied, intermingled and lying on straw. The tops of the lorries were marked with a large Red Cross, and luckily the prowling Jabos left them alone. The hospital was in a school, and held about 400 casualties, including some from the 6th Airborne Division. Merryweather arrived at the hospital the day after his colleagues, and was reunited with Hurst. The patients were looked after by one or two German surgeons, six French doctors and about eighty French nurses; the standard of medical care was described by Trooper Hurst as being 'good'. He added that the food was poor, consisting of nothing but lukewarm coffee for breakfast, black bread and beans for dinner, and pasta in the evening. He was unable to eat due to his condition, and was sustained by intravenous injections.

On 2 August American forces were reported to be close by, and the Germans departed. It took four more days of skirmishing around the town, and some street fighting, in which the Resistance took part, before the city was clear of enemy forces. The hospital was immediately visited by a US Army medical team, and some support troops. The patients were examined, and their wounds re-dressed with proper materials; the German and French staff had been very short of everything, including bandages, swabs and wound pads. More to the point, serious food in the form of US tinned rations, and good, hot strong coffee was supplied while beer, cigarettes and candy were handed out to all and sundry.

The next day, 6 August, a US Army medical unit moved the patients into ambulances for a short but fairly comfort being mortared by their own side, their injuries, and the trauma of being captured so close to safety, and the fear of being summarily shot. They were moved again, to an old monastery being used as a makeshift surgical station. The operating theatre was a large roomable drive to the US 35th Evacuation Hospital, located between Rennes and Fougères. There the two SAS troopers – they had lost contact with Lieutenant Fowles – were injected with penicillin and plied with good food; they were warm, comfortable, and free.

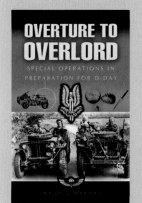

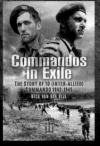

BEHIND ENEMY LINES WITH THE SAS
THE STORY OF AMEDEE MAINGARD, SOE AGENT

Amedee Maingard was a young Mauritian studying in London in 1939 who volunteered for the British Army. After a frustrating spell in the infantry, Maingard joined the SOE. He parachuted into occupied France in 1943 to join the 'Stationer' circuit, initially as radio operator but soon was second-in-command in the circuit, arranging the delivery of weapons, supplies and personnel to the Resistance. After a year's clandestine work, he narrowly escaped the fate of his organiser who was captured by the Germans in May 1944. Undeterred, Maingard developed his own 'Shipwright' circuit in time to support the (FFI) and the arrival of fifty-five men of 1st SAS Regiment for the ill-fated Operation *Bulbasket* shortly after D-Day. Somehow managing to keep the peace among the Gaullists, Communists, British and Americans fighting for the French common cause, Maingard continued his vital work until the liberation of central France, earning recognition from both the British and French governments. *Behind Enemy Lines With the SAS* is more than a story of great bravery and dedication to duty in wartime.

ISBN: 9781844156184 • Hbk • **£19.99**

THE DRUMS OF MEMORY

SAS raids deep behind enemy lines in North Africa; wartime soldiering in the Scots Guards; with SOE dropping by parachute to fight alongside Italian partisans; insights into the high life off duty in Cairo, Beirut and elsewhere; Cold War subterfuge in Europe and the Middle East; twenty-three years as an MP at the heart of British political life. Sir Stephen Hastings MC's rich experiences make this first-class reading.

ISBN: 9780850528084 • Pbk • **£12.95**

FIGHTING MAD
ONE MAN'S GUERRILLA WAR – MICHAEL CALVERT

Michael Calvert was one of the legendary figures of the Second World War. He hit the headlines as 'Mad Mike' after the first Chindit campaign in 1943, with a reputation as a tough and daring leader of guerrilla troops. He was one of the first men selected for the Chindits by the controversial General Orde Wingate. He became Wingate's right-hand man – both in fierce jungle fighting and in battles against stick-in-the-mud staff officers. His speciality was penetrating behind enemy lines. Mad Mike fought in the snow and ice of Norway, in the steaming jungles of Burma, and on the battlefields of Europe where in 1945 he commanded the crack Special Air Service Brigade.

ISBN: 9781844152247 • Pbk • **£12.99**

COMMANDOS IN EXILE
THE STORY OF 10 (INTER-ALLIED) COMMANDO 1942-1945

Formed from members of Free Forces who had escaped from German occupation, 10 (Inter-Allied) Commando was one of the most unusual units in WW2. All members had to pass the Green Beret commando course at Achnacarry in Scotland and the book begins by describing this training. With no less than six national troops, plus X Troop drawn from exiled Jews, 10 Commando never fought as an entity but loaned troops for specific operations, such as 1 Troop (French) taking part in the Dieppe Raid, 2 Troop (Dutch) fighting at Arnhem, 5 Troop (Norwegian) raiding the Lofoten Islands. At other times groups played a key intelligence role questioning POWs, translating captured documents, conducting reconnaissance patrols and intelligence gathering on the D-Day beaches.

ISBN: 9781844157907 • Hbk • **£19.99**

FIGHTING WITH THE COMMANDOS
THE RECOLLECTIONS OF STAN SCOTT NO 3 COMMANDO

Fighting With The Commandos tells what the Second World War was like for a fighting soldier. After enlisting under-age, Stan Scott was 'found out', joined the Home Guard and then a Young Soldiers Unit (for those too young to serve overseas). He managed to get out to Iraq but was again sent home. He then joined 3 Commando led by Brigadier Peter Young and landed on Sword Beach on D-Day. He graphically describes the action thereafter which included being among the first to reach Pegasus Bridge and relieve the glider borne troops under Major John Howard. Plenty of excitement and danger were to follow and readers will revel in a no-holds-barred memoir which points an illuminating picture of life for the rank-and-file in the build-up to the climax of the war.

ISBN: 9781844157747 • Hbk • **£19.99**

GUARDSMAN AND COMMANDO
THE WAR MEMOIRS OF RSM CYRIL FEEBERY DCM

Guardsman and Commando is Cyril Feebery's memoir of his service with the British Army between 1937 and 1945. Feebery served with the Grenadier Guards in the British Expeditionary Force, was evacuated wounded from Dunkirk, completed Commando training in Scotland and joined the Middle East Commando (Layforce). On the disbandment of Layforce, he joined the Folboat Section, later the Special Boat Section, and trained as a canoeist under Captain Roger Keyes VC to conduct commando operations from submarines. When the SBS was later absorbed into the Special Air Service (SAS), Feebery took part in raids on Benghazi and Tripoli. With the creation of the Special Boat Squadron (SBS), Feebery served as Squadron Sergeant Major under Major the Earl Jellicoe. He was captured by Italian forces after a raid on airfields in Sardinia, and later escaped from a Prisoner of War camp in Italy to regain the Allied side. After recovering from malaria, Feebery became Squadron Sergeant Major, Headquarters Squadron, 1st SAS Regiment in 1944. He participated in SAS operations in the Dijon area of France, then in Northern France and Belgium. The manuscript concludes with SAS operations to obtain the surrender of German occupation forces in Norway.

ISBN: 9781844158119 • Hbk • **£19.99**

IN ACTION WITH THE SAS
A SOLDIER'S ODYSSEY FROM DUNKIRK TO BERLIN

Roy Close's wartime experiences make breathtaking reading. Mobilised in 1939 he became part of the BEF and was fortunate to avoid death or captivity during the German blitzkrieg and escape through Dunkirk. Sent to North Africa, he joined the Paras and, from there, to the SAS. In 1944 he operated behind enemy lines with the Maquis in France, who were in open insurrection against the German occupiers. The scene then shifts to Holland and the advance through Germany. He witnessed Paris and Berlin in very early post-war years and was part of the Quadripartite Government of the former German capital.

ISBN: 9781844152865 • Hbk • **£19.99**

TO ORDER PLEASE CALL:
01226 734222

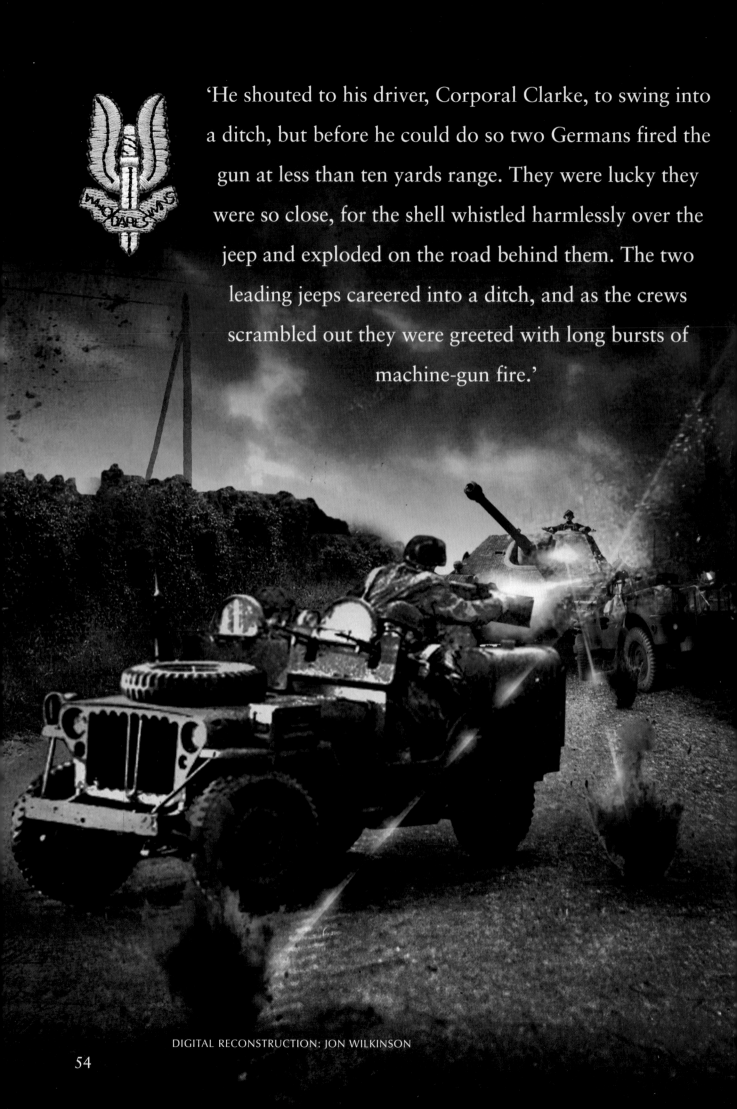

'He shouted to his driver, Corporal Clarke, to swing into a ditch, but before he could do so two Germans fired the gun at less than ten yards range. They were lucky they were so close, for the shell whistled harmlessly over the jeep and exploded on the road behind them. The two leading jeeps careered into a ditch, and as the crews scrambled out they were greeted with long bursts of machine-gun fire.'

SAS IN EUROPE – OPERATION WALLACE 1944

Operation *Wallace* was by far the most ambitious task undertaken by the SAS so far. It was certainly the most imaginative and hazardous. We were to be dropped deep inside the heavily wooded terrain of Central France where we were to carry out mobile guerrilla warfare in which our powerfully armed jeeps were to cause as much chaos and damage as possible to German transport and troops.

By Draper and Challenor

Extracted from *Tanky Challenor* and reproduced by permission of Pen & Sword Books Ltd.

I t was a job I looked forward to with relish. I liked the swashbuckling conception of the operation; ambush the enemy, hit him hard, then disappear at high speed. A sophisticated form of licensed 'mugging'. The SAS had operated behind the enemy lines before but never quite on this scale. David Stirling had carried out several successful sorties in the desert and our sabotage work in Italy had piloted a new form of warfare, but they had been strictly one-off pin-prick operations as there was no re-supply from the air, and as soon as our explosives were expended we had to escape to our own lines.

Major Roy Farran: 'a legend among fighting soldiers'.

As Major Farran put it, '*They could be compared to the behaviour of a naughty boy who knocks on perhaps two doors in a street then runs away.*' This time we were to be supported by the whole weight of Transport Command, and in theory could stay and fight as long as the war lasted and we survived.

Major Farran's squadron, to which I was attached, had its proposed base in the Forest of Chatillon, north of Dijon. The timing was perfect for Operation *Wallace*. General Patton's Third Army had broken clear from the Cherbourg Peninsula while Montgomery, acting as the pivot at Caen, was poised to deliver a long-range right hook at the enemy lines. The Germans were falling back, presenting us with an essential ingredient for the success of the venture – a fluid front through which our small fast jeeps could infiltrate and cause havoc. Every man was fully aware of the risks and dangers

involved, but we were as eager to go as kids embarking on a school outing.

On 19 August our twenty jeeps were driven to an airfield where Dakotas piloted by the British 46th Group were waiting to transport us to France. They were no ordinary jeeps; the upper structure had been removed and each had been specially modified for work in the roughest and toughest conditions. Extra fuel tanks were attached to the side to give them greater range, and there was a larder of tinned food in case anyone was separated from the main group. In addition there were mines, explosives, grenades and a lot of reserve ammunition.

Each member of the three-man crew had a colt .45 and a carbine, but the major difference was in our jeeps' awesome fire power. On the driver's side was a single Vickers-K machine gun capable of firing 1,300 rounds a minute; a twin Vickers was mounted on the front passenger's side, and another twin Vickers, or a .5 Browning at the rear. The ammunition was a mixture of high explosive, tracer,

The American Dakota with British markings. These were used by the RAF to transport specially modified jeeps and equipment, used by the SAS for operations in France.

armour piercing and incendiary. When they all opened fire the effect over a hundred yards was devastating.

I was driver-gunner in the lead jeep of our section. The front passenger seat was occupied by Lieutenant Hugh Gurney, a quietly spoken, tough-as-teak veteran from Cromer, Norfolk; Parachutist Bob Fyffe – nicknamed 'Will' – was rear gunner and wireless operator.

We landed on the only serviceable strip at Rennes airfield which had just been liberated by the Americans and was pock-marked with bomb craters. Within twenty-four hours of landing the column of jeeps was winding its way along the barely discernible tracks in the forests north of Orleans and heading for our prepared base near Chatillon some 150 miles away. The roads were often deep in mud, and at times we had to skirt round pockets of Germans when we were forced to drive across open country. We passed the occasional village where the excited Maquis greeted us as liberators, the first Allied troops they had seen, and naturally they wanted to celebrate, a temptation that was difficult to resist. They also warned Major Farran in which villages there were German troops.

As long as we kept to the maze of narrow country lanes we were reasonably safe, for the Germans tended to keep to metalled roads. Our first mishap occurred when we were crossing a large road near Montargis and one of the jeeps became separated from the column. Our normal tactic was to choose a point where the main road was crossed by a track, send a patrol jeep ahead and when the all clear was given the column roared across at top speed. The patrol jeep then became tail-end Charlie when the column was safely across. On this occasion, however, the patrol car driven by Sergeant Forster carried straight on and lost contact with the rest of us.

Because of constant strafing and bombing by Allied aircraft, the Germans preferred to move by night enabling the SAS to make good progress during the day behind the lines.

Sergeant Forster, realizing his mistake, decided to return to the base in the Forest of Chatillon. On the way he had many exciting adventures, including a collision with a German staff car during which he and his crew killed four high-ranking officers.

We spent the first night concealed in the Forest of Dracy. Although our mission was in its infancy we had already learned that it was best to travel by day as the Germans preferred to move at night because of the continuous strafing and bombing by Allied planes. We made excellent progress and were fifty miles behind the enemy lines and still undetected.

The next morning was largely spent gathering information about enemy movements, and in this respect Captain Ramon Lee, a French officer, proved invaluable. The villagers seemed to sniff us out like dogs scenting a truffle and Ramon was very adept at sifting the genuine from the misleading information.

For the next stage of our journey, Major Farran

A German half track and machine-gunner scanning the terrain for enemy activity.

decided to split the squadron into three sections – eight under him, five under Captain Lee, and the remainder under Lieutenant David Leigh, an officer who had gained considerable experience of jeep operations in the desert. My jeep came under Lieutenant Leigh's command. No one could have a better man in a tight corner, tough, enterprising and totally unflappable.

Major Farran gave orders that each party was to set off at half-hour intervals and follow the same route, although this need not be adhered to if they hit trouble. He emphasised that at this early stage it was preferable to avoid colliding with the enemy. Captain Lee, whose volatile Latin temperament unfortunately over rode the need for caution, accepted some local misinformation that the road ahead was clear and went forward with all the abandon of an old-time cavalry charge, slap into some Germans. He managed to break through, but not before one of his jeeps was knocked out.

Major Farran, not overjoyed at the Frenchman's impetuosity, had no option but to press on and find out what had happened to his unit. An extremely voluble and over-excited local, who saw his role as the spearhead of the newly arrived liberators, jumped on the bonnet of the Major's car and urged him forward. It needed Farran's pistol in his ribs to subdue him, and when he had quietened down he led the unit to a road which wound below a steep cliff. There he jumped down and expressed a desire to go home. Farran also got out, and when he walked round the corner was greeted with a burst of Spandau fire. He dived headfirst into a ditch, and when he peered out he saw about a hundred Germans with horse-drawn vehicles lying in ambush under the trees. It was patently obvious that, though Captain Lee had been able to crash through, there was no chance of his doing so. He had no choice but to withdraw, but not before his men had loosed off a few rounds and set one cart on fire. Retracing his tracks, he left a message with a Frenchman to be passed on to Lieutenant Leigh's unit when it caught up, instructing him to head for a bridge which crossed a river at Merry-sur-Yonne.

We received the message and linked up that night in the Forest of St Jean, over a hundred miles behind the front. There we leaguered for the night near a Priory which had been converted into a farm. In the morning some locals from the village of Chateau Gerard brought us gifts of flowers, wine, butter and eggs.

Farran expressed his anger with a subdued Ramon by reducing his command to two jeeps, although he still allowed him to lead the column, because of his command of French.

Unfortunately a Frenchman of dubious loyalty told Captain Lee that the village of Villaines was clear of the enemy and he ran straight into a group of seasoned Afrika Korps troops. The two jeeps were trapped in a cul-de-sac under heavy fire and a barrage of grenades. Lieutenant Dodds, who was injured when his jeep crashed, was taken prisoner along with Corporal Walsh, who had remained to give covering fire for Captain Lee, and Lieutenant Lord John Manners, who managed to break clear.

Major Farran, some distance behind and with no idea what had happened, drove straight into an ambush. As he turned a corner he found himself looking down the muzzle of a seventy-five millimetre gun. He shouted to his driver, Corporal Clarke, to swing into a ditch, but before he could do so two Germans fired the gun at less than ten yards range. They were lucky they were so close for the shell whistled harmlessly over the jeep and exploded on the road behind them. The two leading jeeps careered into a ditch, and as the crews scrambled out they were greeted with long bursts of machine-gun fire. Farran peeped over the top of the ditch and saw the detached spare wheel from one of the jeeps rolling down the road pursued by yelling Germans firing automatic weapons. As they were crawling away from Farran's wrecked jeep. Lieutenant Carpendale, the Signals Officer, remembered he had left his operational maps and codes behind and he went back with Corporal Clarke to retrieve them. When they reached a convenient gully they set up the Bren they had managed to retain and opened fire while Farran ran back through a gauntlet of fire to warn the rest of us who were following up. The Germans were belting down the road firing as they advanced, and one particularly big and blond soldier with a Schmeisser called upon the Major to surrender. Farran fired his carbine and saw him drop. When he reached the two jeeps led by Lieutenant Jim Mackie, he guided him to a convenient lane from where their guns could fire at short

> 'The two jeeps were trapped in a cul-de-sac under heavy fire and a barrage of grenades.'

THE BREN GUN

Calibre:	.303 inch
Muzzle velocity:	2,440 ft/s
Rate of fire:	500 rpm
Unloaded weight:	10.15 kg
Cooling:	Air

ILLUSTRATION: JON WILKINSON

range into the German flank. Sergeant Major Mitchell, with ten men with carbines and four Brens, was posted to the left while Farran held the centre with two more jeeps. Ahead of them. Corporal Clarke was still banging away with his Bren. By now it had developed into a pitched battle with the Germans, who were able to call up mortar and artillery fire. Unwisely the Germans decided to make a charge along both sides of the road, giving the Paras a golden opportunity to open fire at less than fifty yards range. The Jerries were knocked down like skittles in an alley, with Mackie's troops accounting for a whole platoon which tried to advance across an open field. Despite the heavy casualties, the Germans pressed on with their foolhardy attack and were cut down from all three sides. By now Clarke's Bren had ceased firing and Farran feared he had been captured or killed. Clarkie had been captured, but not for long. The German who was leading him to captivity at the muzzle end of his Schmeisser slipped on the river bank and fell into a deep pool, dropping his gun. Clarke made off at full speed and managed to link up with Captain Lee some days later.

Meanwhile, after an hour's hectic fighting, the SAS men were in a desperate situation: the Germans had managed to infiltrate their rear and set up a mortar and machine-gun attack. Farran realized that unless

A German mortar crew in action.

> 'Meanwhile, after an hour's hectic fighting, the SAS men were in a desperate situation: the Germans had managed to infiltrate their rear and set up a mortar and machine-gun attack.'

Lieutenant Leigh turned up soon he had no alternative but to withdraw or be wiped out. He also feared that we had been so slow in turning up because we had heard the intense firing and veered off in another direction. So under cover of Lieutenant Mackie's guns he withdrew down a small lane which unfortunately turned out to be a dead-end leading to a mill. The trailer containing the vital wireless equipment was destroyed in the withdrawal, making their plight even worse. But he and his men with the assistance of two locals, Monsieur and Madame Defour, managed to make their way over a stream and across country to link up with a narrow rutted lane near the village of Jeux. There a farm labourer warned him that the entire area was crawling with Germans including a Panzer division, fortunately without its armour. Making a wide detour he set off in the direction of the SAS base commanded by Captain Grant Hibbert, but a blaze of headlights which indicated a large enemy convoy forced him to slip into the forest, switch off all lights and wait until the last vehicle had passed. There he wondered what in the name of God had happened to my unit led by Lieutenant Leigh.

We had not, as he imagined, veered off and sought a safer route. When the fighting broke out in Villaines we were more than two miles astern and did not hear a thing. What did arouse my concern was a terrible smell which prompted me to remark to Lieutenant Gurney, 'Blimey, there's a broken sewer around here somewhere.' He replied with what was almost a dismissive sneer at my gastronomic ignorance, 'Tanky, you don't know a good cheese when it's under your nose.' I had forgotten he was something of a connoisseur, and that we were passing through an area renowned for its cheese. 'Will' Fyffe piped up from the rear, 'I'd trade all the cheese in the world for a dram of decent whisky.'

Our conversation was an indication of how relaxed we were and how oblivious to what our comrades ahead were being subjected to. Yet behind the badinage we were extremely alert and looking for the slightest sign of danger. As we approached the village we could see no sign of the enemy, then suddenly from the cover of some trees on the side of the road all hell broke loose. The Germans had been lying in wait for us, informed by a collaborator that the squadron was in three sections. In Italy betrayal was virtually unknown, whereas in France it was far from uncommon – for too many the Occupation was more welcomed than resistance, and frequently the Resistance was penetrated by pro-German elements whose role was to betray them and the Allied forces working behind the lines. They were as despised by loyal Frenchmen as they were by us, and when they were caught their countrymen showed no mercy. You had a better chance of survival if you were a German.

My first impression was that we had run into an entire

The bodies German troops who had bunched together and were cut down by gunfire.

German Division, but once the initial shock was over we hit back with every gun we had in a desperate attempt to make sure our line of withdrawal was not cut. Almost immediately Lieutenant Leigh was shot in the head and dragged clear of the jeep by two of the crew while his driver. Corporal McEachon, continued to fire the Vickers over the steering wheel. At the same time I nipped out of my own jeep to take up position behind a tree to deal with a file of Germans working slowly along our flank. The American carbine I carried was an accurate and lethal weapon and I dropped the three leading Jerries with the same number of rounds. The remainder scampered off, and I pumped more rounds into the bodies of the prostrate Germans just to make sure they would take no further part in the action. When I looked round I saw that McEachon was sprawled across the jeep with blood pumping from a wound in his throat. I waited for a pause in the firing, then sprinted across to his jeep, slung him on my back and carried him to my own vehicle. My tunic was soaked with his blood.

Lieutenant Gurney, who had assumed command now Lieutenant Leigh was wounded, decided there was no hope of forcing our way through the village and he ordered the jeeps to be turned round so that we could escape. We managed to do so but found that one jeep was so badly damaged it would have to be destroyed. This was done with a grenade dropped into the petrol tank.

As we drove off like bats out of hell, 'Will' Fyffe leaned across and told me that McEachon was dead. We drove on until we found a ditch by a mill that was

> 'I pumped more rounds into the bodies of the prostrate Germans just to make sure they would take no further part in the action.'

one huge blaze of wild flowers, and there we laid him gently on the ground, removed his pay book and dog-tag, hoping the Maquis would find him and give him a decent burial. Although Jerry was in hot pursuit we paused long enough for Lieutenant Gurney to offer up a simple prayer while the rest of us stood heads bowed with our berets in our hands. When we moved off I was too choked to speak, McEachon had been such a close friend.

As we had lost wireless contact with Major Farran, Lieutenant Gurney decided to try and link up with Ramon Lee. By now Lieutenant Leigh was in a very bad way and we decided his only hope of survival was with the Maquis so he was taken at great risk to the home of a well-known member in Eppoise who moved him to a hospital where he died a short time later.

We drove off in the dark and were deluged by a thunderstorm of monsoon dimensions, and soon I was shivering from a bout of malaria. I had suffered an earlier bout for which a French farmer had prescribed a local remedy they called Mirabella, a type of pure spirit made from the fermented juice of small plums. Though it was effective, it had the unfortunate and unwanted effect of making

The French Marquis giving recruits weapons training. The Frenchman on the left is holding a British Sten gun.

Paddy Mayne's unit under fire in a forest near Coppenburg during the advance into Germany 1945.

me as tipsy as a sailor on a jaunt ashore, but that was infinitely better than being a burden to my comrades, and in any case a little Dutch courage never did anyone a great deal of harm. Lots of men have distinguished themselves in battle with a mild hangover.

As we entered a village in driving and blinding rain, we were engaged by Germans who were there in some considerable force, and in the pitch darkness and mounting confusion my own jeep and two others got bogged down on the perimeter. One jeep in each unit towed a trailer for additional supplies and equipment,

and mine was the unfortunate one. We jumped out and tried to release it in order to facilitate turning the vehicle in the narrow road, but because of the rumble of thunder and the crackle of gunfire we did not hear the order to destroy it and withdraw to the remaining jeeps. It was so dark and the rain so heavy that visibility was down to zero and we decided to hole up outside the village and wait till conditions improved. Unbeknown to us, as the main part of our group pulled out of one end of the village the Germans withdrew from the other and Lieutenant Gurney, Lieutenant Birtwhistle (who had been wounded) and a couple of the lads decided to go back and retrieve two of the abandoned jeeps, leaving behind mine with its trailer.

When dawn broke we managed to contact a civilian, and one Para from Jersey who spoke fluent French was able to discover that the enemy had gone. I thought: What a turn up for the book! We've got to go back and retrieve my jeep which has a wireless we can't work, then set off to find the others who could be anywhere. We managed to get the jeep out without any further trouble and then held a council of war to decide our next move. We devised a simple plan: if we encountered any soft stuff – trucks, staff cars, petrol tankers – we would blast them with every available gun.

Tanky and jeep in the village of L'Isle-sur-Sereine.

If we met any armoured units we would drive straight through with our right arms raised in the Nazi salute, and our left crossing ourselves in prayer. It wasn't a counsel of despair, just another example of our almost boyish sense of humour. The rain stopped and it turned into a beautiful day as we drove at a leisurely pace towards L'lsle-sur-Sereine where we hoped to get a friendly reception and pick up some useful information. It was a largish village, and as we approached it I called to my mates, *'Stand by for a ripe load of bleeding trouble.'* But there was no need for the warning. Men, women and children came streaming towards us waving and cheering and pelting us with flowers. Men tried to greet us with one hand while holding out a bottle with the other. Several of the local Maquis clambered aboard brandishing their guns and clapping us on the back. I was astonished to see people taking photographs. The local leader informed us that a grand meal was being prepared for us; good news that was tempered by the disappointment that he had no information as to the whereabouts of the rest of the column.

As the senior ranker, I had to make a vital decision: press on or remain and enjoy the proffered hospitality. I decided on the latter. Even by peace-time standards the meal was excellent and the wine flowed like tap water. There was more posing for photographs which was followed by long speeches which I could not understand. Not that I cared, for by now I had progressed to the

brandy. Glasses were raised in toasts to victory and with the French-speaking Jersey man acting as interpreter I proposed;
'Cobblers to the Führer'.

THE FINAL PARADE

At the end of the war the SAS' operational units gradually filtered back to their headquarters base in England, now at Wivenhoe in Essex. Most of the men were demobbed to return to civilian life while the regulars were posted back to the regiments from which they had originally volunteered. Against the Service itself old jealousies now gathered strength and it was eventually deemed there was no need for such a specialist and elitist unit in the post-war army. By October, 1945, the Special Air Service Brigade, with all its constituent units, was ordered to be disbanded.

October 1945, the 'final' parade of 1st and 2nd SAS Regiments at Hylands House, Chelmsford.

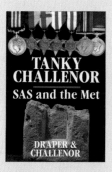

High-quality young officers were arriving, including such SAS 'greats' as Captain the Hon John Slim, Captain Johnny Watts and Peter de la Billiere, all of whom were eventually to command 22 SAS. The morale of the Regiment soared.'

THE SAS ARISES AGAIN – THE MALAYAN EMERGENCY

Less than a year after the SAS had been officially disbanded in October 1945, the War Office instigated an enquiry into the future role, if any, of the special forces. As a result it was decided that no matter to what extent methods of conducting war might change, there would always be a need for small parties of well-trained and well-handled men operating behind the enemy lines.

By John Simpson with Mark Adkin

Extracted from *The Quiet Operator* and reproduced by permission of Pen & Sword Books Ltd.

The Special Air Service filled the above War Office requirement; however, the times were not judged right for the introduction of another regiment into the Regular Army, and so a compromise was reached in the form of an SAS Territorial regiment. It was to be designated 21 SAS. The number 21 was arrived at by a convoluted army method and the new regiment was formed under Lieutenant Colonel Franks, who had commanded 2 SAS in North-West Europe. He had as his second-in-command Major L E O T Hart who had been DA and QMG to the SAS Brigade, and he was followed in command by such stalwarts as Lapraik and Sutherland.

When recruiting commenced in September 1947 a number of ex-SAS personnel volunteered, and these provided the Regiment with a wealth of experience at the outset. A decision was taken to merge with the Artists' Rifles which had been an Officer Cadet Training Unit. The merger resulted in the new unit's official title of 21 SAS (Artists) TA, and until 1950 it was a part of the Army Air Corps.

Two further SAS regiments were formed in the next few years. The first of these, 22 SAS, had a typically ad hoc origin. In 1959 another Territorial SAS regiment numbered 23 was launched. There was also 63 (SAS) Signal Squadron manned by men of the Royal Signals, which provided basic signal back-up for the Territorial regiments, and a reserve squadron, R, as a means of recruiting men for 22 SAS in times of emergency. The genesis of 22 SAS was in the Malayan emergency.

'When recruiting commenced in September 1947 a number of ex-SAS personnel volunteered, and these provided the Regiment with a wealth of experience at the outset.'

A bus which has been ambushed and blown up by Communist Bandits.

BANDITS

In 1948 the Malayan Emergency burst on an unprepared British Army. By 1950 communist insurgents, the majority from the predominantly communist Malayan Peoples' Anti-Japanese Army, had inflicted substantial casualties: 863 civilians, 323 police officers and 154 soldiers. Road travel was risky except with an armed convoy, and the CTs (Communist Terrorists) had seriously disrupted the all-important rubber and tin industries.

The task of creating a special military force to take on the terrorists at their own game, living deep in the jungle for weeks or months at a time, was given to a tough, hard-fighting, hard-drinking sapper officer called Calvert, then on the staff in Hong Kong. Calvert, who had earned a double Blue at Oxford, had gained the soubriquet 'Mad Mike' for some of his less conventional activities. During the war he had had a distinguished, if unusual, career in the Burmese jungle both as a Column Commander and Brigade Commander in Orde Wingate's Chindits. He had also commanded the SAS Brigade in North-West Europe for the last ten months of the war.

The first squadron, A Squadron, was a very mixed bag, including many of whom regular battalions were only too glad to see the back; the hard cases, many of whom had seen substantial service in military detention barracks – even ten deserters from the French Foreign Legion – were taken without hesitation. There was also good material. Veterans from SOE, the original SAS,

Michael Calvert, a tough and hard fighting officer.

Orde Wingate.

Force 136 and Ferret Force, men with outstanding war records responded. Among them were two officers who were to be the architects of the SAS as they are known today. The lean, thoughtful brewer's son from Devon, John Woodhouse, who, as SAS legend has it, lived on a tin of sardines a day, and a bespectacled Suffolk clergyman's son, Dare Newell, who had seen service behind enemy lines with SOE in Albania and Malaya. It was the latter who was subsequently to be known by the affectionate and well-deserved nickname of Godfather to the SAS.

Much credit is due to Calvert for his concept of operations, and in creating the Regiment, but his name is inevitably associated in SAS eyes with the inauspicious beginnings of 22 SAS, together with the many problems that flowed from it in the years to come. Calvert's administrative difficulties with his widely scattered Regiment were enormous and were aggravated by his personal refusal to doff his cap to authority. This was part of the reason that he never really won the confidence and backing of his superior headquarters.

His large, imperturbable Adjutant, Pat Winter, an officer who found it hard to fit into the ceremonial routine of the peacetime Scots Guards, did his best to protect his Commanding Officer from himself. Calvert had recruited him in an aeroplane from Hong Kong at the height of an electrical storm. As Winter has said, when Calvert disliked some administrative problem his solution was usually to collect half a dozen of the blokes and disappear into the *ulu* [jungle] for a couple of weeks. By the middle of 1951 Calvert had shot his bolt. He was a sick man. He had driven himself mercilessly for twelve years, even his champion boxer and front row forward physique, plus his obsessive determination to keep going, was finally defeated. He was invalided back to England suffering from Malaria, dysentery, hookworm and the general depredations of extreme climates.

MAJOR LEN WILLMOTT

Brigadier Michael Calvert was replaced by a burly, 6'4" Highlander called John Sloane who had no experience whatever of special forces or irregular warfare. His task was to sort out this unruly, far from popular, fledgling regiment. Early in his tenure of command he sent one of his squadron commanders, John Woodhouse, at Woodhouse's instigation, back to England to establish a recruiting and selection system more in keeping with SAS principles. It was a move that laid the foundations of the present-day rigorous procedure.

It was at this point that the quiet, self-effacing new Signals Officer arrived. Len Willmott had given his new job much thought on the long, uncomfortable journey out on a converted Lancaster bomber. He was returning at last to where he believed he belonged. On the train from Singapore to the then SAS base at Kluang in Johore he gazed with interest at the matted undergrowth, towering trees that flanked the railway track which gave fleeting glimpses of the jungle canopy stretching interminably to the horizon on either side.

At Kluang station there was no one to meet him. He thought it strange, but perhaps his signal had not got through. Clearly, from what he had seen, communications in this sort of environment were probably difficult. After some prudent negotiations he found a taxi to take him to the SAS camp.

His arrival appalled him. Irregular soldier though he was, his first impression came as a shock. The sentry at the gate was smoking and failed to salute. Len asked the way to the Officers' Mess, only to be given grudging, surly directions. Perhaps he was asking too much, but in reality he knew from the moment he entered the camp that things were wrong, although he was unaware of the origins of the Malayan Scouts, or what had gone before during the last few hectic months. There was a noisy alcoholic party going on in the Mess, so he sought out the Mess Sergeant and got himself installed in a tent. It had been a strangely disappointing day, not just because he had not found what he expected, but because he could not reconcile what he had found in Malaya with what he had seen of the original SAS in Egypt in 1941.

Len Willmott, September 1944.

The next morning Len reported to the Adjutant, as required of all newly-arrived officers. He remembers Winter as large, welcoming, a bit distant, and preoccupied. Winter was indeed preoccupied. Loyal as he was to Calvert, he knew that things were very wrong. The Regiment's communications were a shambles and Len's predecessor had earned himself the nickname 'Spanner'; if it were possible for anything to go wrong 'Spanner' made certain that it did. Central to the problem in 1952 was that no one seriously expected the wireless to work in the jungle. If patrols or outstations managed to get through on their sets it was a bonus.

Communications were only one of the Adjutant's worries. His principal preoccupation was translating into practical form Sloane's efforts to transform a rabble into some sort of military order. The quiet new Signal Officer made little impression on him at the time, apart from the fact that he was polite, well turned out, and did not add to his problems.

Len first drew attention to himself over the matter of drill parades or, more precisely, the Signals Officer's absence from the first Adjutant's Parade. Drill as a panacea of all evils is deeply ingrained in any guardsman's soul and, as part of the Sloane sorting-out process. Winter had ordered a series of RSM's and Adjutant's drill parades. They were a disaster. On the first RSM's parade B Squadron did not show up at all. On the Adjutant's parade there was a distinct shortage of officers, and, in the middle of it, the Rhodesian Squadron decided it was not for them, turned smartly to their right and marched off. Winter vented his rage on the officers who had failed to parade, only to be told politely but firmly by Len that, counting his Other Rank

Officers of the 22 SAS, Sungei Besi Camp, Malaya, 1952. Left front row, end, Major Len Willmott; next to him is Captain Pat Winter. Centre of row, seated Lieutenant Colonel 'Tod' Sloane.

service as half (as he was entitled to do), he was in fact the senior of the two. As the orders had only specified officers junior to the Adjutant, he had not paraded. He detected a glint of amusement in the small man's clear gaze as Len added, *'perhaps drill parades are not what's needed to knock this lot into shape'.* A roar of laughter erupted from Winter's vast frame. RSM's and Adjutant's parades passed into history.

Len set about learning and solving the complications of signalling in Malaya. Conditions for good wireless reception could hardly have been worse. Mountains, trees and atmospherics combined to make clear communications the remote exception rather than the rule. During the monsoon, for example, there were daily thunderstorms with continuous flashes of lightning and thunder lasting up to an hour.

Then there were difficulties with the wireless itself. The main patrol set was a tropicalised version of the pre-war 18 set. It was bulky, burdensome, and many signallers of that day believed that the best way of tuning the transmitter to a recalcitrant receiver was to kick it. It also required a heavy dry battery, the useful life of which was short and unpredictable. SAS patrols, deep in the jungle for weeks and months on end, had either to have a regular supply of new batteries by air, thus compromising their

> 'Next thing you know you are floating through the air, and it's one of the most wonderful feelings in the world; then you see the trees coming.'

whereabouts, or take on patrol the even larger 62 set designed for vehicles. It was not the weight of the set so much as having to take accumulator batteries with a pedal generating machine to recharge them.

The British strategic plan to deny the jungle terrorists food, a product of Calvert's fertile mind, was beginning to take effect, driving the CTs further and further into the jungle, many miles from habitation, thus forcing them to clear areas of jungle to grow food. These were easily spotted from the air. Shortly after Len's arrival plans were made to attack a complex of CT gardens in the far North of Malaya near the Thai border; it was called the Belum Valley operation. To achieve surprise, the SAS decided that one squadron would parachute in. The distances and terrain gave the Signals Officer formidable communications problems, but it was the concept of jumping into the jungle (tree jumping) that was the real unknown, especially for the operators jumping with the cumbersome sets. The theory was simple.

You selected a suitable tree as you approached the jungle canopy, praying your parachute would snag in the upper branches. A hundred feet of rope was provided for each man with which to abseil to the ground. In practice it was more as described by Major John Salmon, the second-in-command of 22 SAS:

> *'Next thing you know you are floating through the air, and it's one of the most wonderful feelings in the world; then you see the trees coming. You are coming down beautifully steering for the middle of the trees. The hot air makes you swing violently, as if a giant had caught hold of you. You let the air spill out of the chute and look for a good, healthy tree. Sometimes you make that spot; often you don't. It's hard to tell until you are a few feet away. When you hit a tree you don't know whether you will stay there or not. Often the branch snaps so you hurtle down, smashing into the branches on the way, until you finally come to a halt. If it holds, then you know you are safe.*

Although there were no casualties on the Belum Valley operation and tree jumping became an SAS speciality, it soon came to be regarded for what it was, a dangerous way to descend. Casualties mounted, including one horrific occasion when an NCO, in agony with his harness twisted round his private parts, cut himself free and dropped 150 feet to his death.

Without fuss Len set about putting the signals right with the help of the vastly experienced Sergeant Steve Stevenson. Slowly, Winter began to take note of this quiet, almost shy officer. The standard of communications improved

An SAS soldier makes a safe landing after a successful jump into the jungle canopy.

TREE JUMPING

Tree jumping was a rapid way of dropping troops into a target area. The parachute canopy would catch in the tree tops enabling the trooper to abseil quickly into the jungle.

to put the Regiment's administration on a proper footing and take over responsibility for in-theatre recruitment and training. So the long haul back to SAS standards got under way. Coincidentally Len came directly under Dare's command, and the job of MTO (Motor Transport Officer) when it became vacant. There was no replacement immediately available so Len acquired the job in addition to his own. The traffic-accident returns dropped markedly, and officers found it increasingly difficult to get hold of jeeps for private purposes. As usual Len always seemed to be about when needed; if there was a driver short Len would drive the ration lorry or the water truck, if a patrol was due out of the jungle on to a road that ran through a 'black' (terrorist-dominated) area Len invariably took the convoy out himself.

The Adjutant's first real clash with Len came over a Court Martial. A Rhodesian trooper had refused a parachute jump – a court-martial offence in any airborne unit. The trooper was entitled by law to — and needed – a defending officer. He was also one of the Rhodesian Squadron signallers so he asked for Len to defend him because 'he looked after his blokes'.

'That bloody man, Len,' said Winter years later; *'He went through the SOPs (Standard Operational Procedures) with a fine tooth-comb and found one discrepancy in them. I'd presented an open-and-shut case as Prosecuting Officer, and bloody Willmott got up and said there was "No case to answer".'*

The Rhodesian got off. Winter was glad he did in retrospect as he redeemed himself later. Winter apart, the Rhodesian Squadron Commander, Peter Wall, afterwards to become a Lieutenant General and Chief of the Defence Staff in the Rhodesian Armed Forces, was furious.

Life in 22 SAS continued to be eventful. Colonel Sloane was relieved in mid-1953 by Lieutenant Colonel Oliver Brooke of the Manchester Regiment, another Regular soldier with no experience of special forces but very different from Sloane. Brooke was a fierce, quick-tempered extrovert, more than a match for the still intractable members of the SAS. The evening before he was due to assume command a group of NCOs and men, who had imbibed not too wisely in the town, decided to wake up the new Commanding Officer. They let off an explosive charge outside the Officers' Mess, the destructive effect of which they clearly underestimated. It blew down the wall. The table next to which Brooke was standing took off and landed about twenty feet away. Dare Newell was standing next to Brooke and the outgoing Commanding Officer, Sloane, while Len was sitting in a corner sipping a beer and recalls:

'I hit the deck like everyone else but, bugger me, there were Brooke, Sloane and Dare still standing and chatting away as if nothing had happened.'

dramatically, even though, as is the lot of all signals officers, they get precious little credit for it, and plenty of brickbats when the wireless does not work. Len remained unobtrusive, but if there was a signals breakdown in one of the jungle forts Len got there somehow to put it right. He was indefatigable in getting new and better wireless sets, repairing existing ones, and going to endless trouble to train the operators to give them confidence in their equipment. He could also be demanding, requiring reasons in writing if a patrol was out of communication for more than forty-eight hours.

Dare Newell, then a sabre squadron commander, also noted the improvements. He had heard about Len Willmott while he was in Albania, and it was he who had suggested that Len might make a suitable signals officer for 22 SAS. He was to comment many years later,

'Len was the best bloody signals officer we ever had, and SAS communications would have been much better, much sooner, had he stayed with us longer.'

Dare Newell was transferred to Headquarters Squadron

Next day, a Sunday, Brooke took over command officially. Within a couple of hours he had sacked sixteen NCOs and troopers. They were out of camp an hour later. This was what the SAS needed. Unfortunately it was not to last long. Brooke suffered appalling injuries on a tree jump and was flown home to England to spend many months in hospital. Not long afterwards Dare Newell was posted back to England to set up the first SAS staff representation in the War Office, a single grade III staff officer. It was the only staff representation the SAS was to have for many years. Len was promoted Acting Major and took over Headquarter Squadron with responsibility for administration, signals, transport, supplies and, most important, in-theatre selection and training.

As Winter said, '*You hardly noticed Len. HQ Squadron just ran, and he was always around when needed.*' It was a job Len relished. He had been well trained and briefed by Newell and he could put into practice many of the things he had learned from the New Zealanders in Greece, and had thought about ever since his first exposure to the SAS in Kabrit ten or more years earlier.

Newell undoubtedly knew something about Len's SOE background and his wartime career, but Winter had not the slightest idea that he had a distinguished SOE record behind him until 1989. 'I took him as a good but straight-up-and-down signal officer. He never spoke of the war.'

Johnny Cooper, one of Stirling's originals and his driver and gunner in the desert (later Lieutenant Colonel John Cooper MBE DCM MM), was MTO when Len arrived, and a sabre squadron commander for the rest of Len's tour, had no idea either. Both served with Len for two years in Malaya. To 22 SAS in Malaya he was just 'a quiet little bloke who did a good job'.

With the SAS taking shape according to Stirling's principles, and the gradual weeding out of undesirable and unsuitable officers and men, Len really felt he was back where he belonged. The quality of recruits arriving in Malaya from John Woodhouse's embryo organization in England was improving with each intake. High-quality young officers were arriving, including such SAS 'greats' as Captain the Hon John Slim (later Colonel the Viscount Slim OBE), Captain Johnny Watts (later Lieutenant General Sir John Watts, KBE, MC and bar) and 'DLB' (now General Sir Peter de la Billiere, KCB, KBE, DSO, MC and bar), all of whom were eventually to command 22 SAS. The morale of the Regiment soared.

LIVING OFF THE LAND - 1958

Extracted from *The Malayan Emergency*
By Robert Jackson

One of the more notable operations was carried out in February by D Squadron of the 22nd Special Air Service Regiment, commanded by Major Harry Thompson of the Royal Highland Fusiliers. Their target was a ruthless terrorist called Ah Hoi, who was known to the police as the 'baby killer' because he had once slashed with his knife the pregnant wife of a man he believed to be an informer.

Hor Lung, second in command to Chin Peng, surrendered to the security forces and persuaded his former terrorist associates to cease armed resistance.

Chin Peng commander of the MCP

The base of Ah Hoi and his group of bandits was in a large coastal swamp area, 18 miles by 10, north of Telok Anson in Selangor, from where they emerged periodically to terrorize the local rubber estates. The continuing threat they presented caused large numbers of Security Forces personnel to be tied down on guard duties around the plantations, and so the SAS was called in to deal with them once and for all.

Major Thompson planned to use two troops of his thirty-seven-strong force to flush out Ah Hoi, holding the other two troops and his small tactical HQ in readiness to attack once the terrorists were located. The two spearhead troops were dropped from a Blackburn Beverley transport aircraft into the jungle canopy near the western edge of the swamp, suffering one serious casualty when the parachute canopy of one trooper collapsed and he landed heavily, breaking his back (he was evacuated by helicopter).

The plan called for D Squadron to patrol eastwards towards the heart of the swamp, which involved wading through rust-brown water and glutinous, stinking mud, infested by leeches and overgrown with mangroves. The brown stain in the water was caused by iron, and it is interesting to note that because of this, SAS medical staff believed that patrolling through swamp country for lengthy periods actually resulted in less sickness than did normal jungle patrolling.

The spearhead patrol, led by Captain (later Brigadier) Peter de la Billière, spent ten days moving along the line of the Tengi River, picking up occasional small signs that terrorists had passed that way. Sometimes they waded neck-deep in the marsh channels, at others they swam in open water. At night they slept in hammocks slung between trees, or on improvised rafts if no suitable trees were available. Each man carried enough food for fourteen days, as there was no possibility of being re-supplied by air.

On the eighth day the second troop, led by Sergeant Sandilands, sighted two terrorists and opened fire on them, wounding one. Following the wounded man's trail, they found a CT camp about four miles into the swamp and radioed its position, whereupon Major Thompson put the two remaining troops into the swamp from the eastern side. A military and police cordon was also placed around the whole area, this operation taking ten days.

The spearhead SAS patrols had now been in the swamp for three weeks and were reduced to living off the land. Some of the men were in a bad way from exhaustion, the debilitating effects of leeches and ulcerated wounds caused by thorns. Then a frail, sickly girl emerged from the swamp and approached the police cordon with Ah Hoi's offer of surrender; he wanted £3,500 for each of his gang and freedom for those already in prison. She was told to go back to him with the simple message: either surrender within twenty-four hours or be killed in the swamp.

Ah Hoi duly emerged with two CTs. Meanwhile, Major Thompson led a troop after the girl, who had promised to lead them to the remaining terrorists, but she was so exhausted by starvation and disease that she was unable to continue. Thompson therefore held his troop at the edge of the swamp until seven more terrorists surrendered a couple of days later.

> 'The spearhead SAS patrols had now been in the swamp for three weeks and were reduced to living off the land. Some of the men were in a bad way from exhaustion, the debilitating effects of leeches and ulcerated wounds caused by thorns.'

In Negri Sembilan, Operation *Latimer South* was halted for most of the year while Police Special Branch officers carried out their own operations in the area. The biggest success of 1958 was in Johore, where 160 terrorists were persuaded to give themselves up following the defection of the former State Committee Member, Hor Lung, who on 5 April 1958, after years of eluding the Security Forces and on one occasion narrowly escaping death in an air attack, calmly walked into the hamlet of Kampong Tengah and surrendered to a policeman.

Hor Lung was promised huge rewards if he would persuade his former colleagues to turn themselves in, and he obliged beyond the wildest dreams of Special Branch. His own surrender had been kept so secret that not a single terrorist knew that it had happened, and when he returned to the jungle on police instructions, visiting each CT branch and committee in turn, they had no reason to disbelieve him when he informed them that, due to a change in policy, armed resistance was to cease. One by one he led the scattered terrorist groups out of the jungle, until after four months of patient work the Malayan Government announced the surrender of 132 rank-and-file terrorists, plus 28 hard-core unit commanders who were put on show to prove it. It was the biggest mass surrender of the Emergency, and for Chin Peng it was a catastrophe of enormous proportions.

'The longest, most important and most fruitful work that the SAS was to do in South Arabia resulted from their presence throughout the Dhofar war, which lasted, as far as the SAS were concerned, from 1970 until 1976.'

PHOTOGRAPH: VIA IAN GARDINER AUTHOR OF *IN SERVICE OF THE SULTAN*.

SOUTH ARABIA – 1958 TO 1976

In the course of SAS operations in Malaya, and later in Borneo, there were two brief interruptions during which a squadron was engaged in fighting – as opposed to training – in South Arabia. The first occurred in 1958, and the second in 1964. The area of these operations was the Sultanate of Muscat and Oman – an independent state ruled by the Sultan and having long-standing treaties of friendship and co-operation with Britain and the Aden Protectorate.

By Willian Seymour

Extracted from *British Special Forces* and reproduced by permission of Pen & Sword Books Ltd.

Oman, the largest state in the Persian Gulf, is approximately the size of England and Scotland with a population then of not much over half a million. It is of great stategic importance to the West because, situated on the south-east corner of the Arabian peninsula, with its northern point commanding the Hormuz Strait, it controls the corridor through which flows much of the non-Communist oil.

The topography of the Sultanate varies considerably. In the north, where the boundary was then with the Trucial Oman States (now the United Arab Emirates), there is a formidable mountain range running north-east to south-west, with the 10,000 feet Jebel Akhdar (Green Mountain) the highest point; in the west the desert of Oman borders that of the Rub al Khali (the Empty Quarter); the coastline of almost 1,000 miles has a flat plain up to 10 miles wide in places; in the south-west is the province of Dnofar, separated from northern Oman by 400 miles of desert, whose people have a different cultural and social background from the Arabs and Baluchis of the north. The climate is one of extremes: on the coastal plain the temperature at night can be well over 100 degrees Fahrenheit, while in the mountains it can drop so quickly as to freeze the water in a soldier's water-bottle – and always in the mountains there is a wind. Predominantly Oman is a harsh land, but there are fertile areas.

The origin of the trouble which brought D Squadron of the SAS hurrying from Malaya in November 1958 went back a long way, but more immediately to 1952. In that year the Saudis occupied the Buraimi oasis, a fruitful and strategically-valuable tract of land on the Abu Dhabi border, and partly owned by the Sultan of Oman. It was three years before they were evicted, and by then they had spent a lot of time and money undermining the Sultan's authority. Oman is fruitful ground for subversion; it has had a blood-thirsty and

'Oman is fruitful ground for subversion; it has had a blood-thirsty and turbulent history with piracy and land grabbing from without, and tribal rebellion from within.'

71

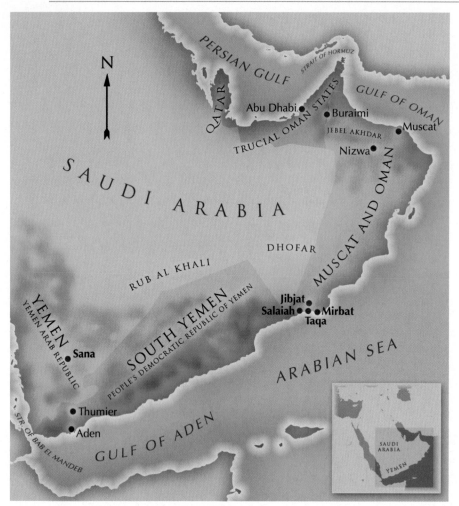

SOUTH ARABIA

turbulent history with piracy and land grabbing from without, and tribal rebellion from within. Murders and acts of treachery have left their curse and vendetta behind – and many of these have been connected with the Imams. These spiritual heads of the country have not always been good and pious men; the Sultan's authority has frequently been challenged by the Imam of the day, as it was in the mid-fifties.

By the time the Saudis had been expelled from Buraimi the old Imam, a friend of the Sultan's, had died and the new one, Ghalib bin Alt, was very much influenced by the Saudis. He himself was a weak man, but he had an extremely strong, intelligent and ambitious brother, Talib, and the two of them lost no time in engaging in active opposition to the Sultan. Moreover, they enlisted two important allies in Suleiman bin Himyar, Lord of the Jebel Akhdar, and the powerful Sheikh Salih bin Isa. In 1955 the Imam, backed by the Saudis, was in dispute with the Sultan over oil rights, and the Sultan settled the matter in December with his British-officered Muscat and Oman Field Force. Ghalib abdicated, Talib escaped to Saudi Arabia, and the Lord of the Green Mountain gave insincere gages of loyalty and retired to the top of his mountain.

But in little over a year the principals were together again; and Talib was now at the head of a strong band of guerrillas whom he had trained with Saudi instructors

while in exile. The brothers raised the standard of revolt, and aided by Sheikh Suleiman completely destroyed the Muscat and Oman Field Force. At this juncture the Sultan requested British aid, which was immediately forthcoming, and a company of the Cameronians and the Trucial Oman Scouts, aided by the RAF, recaptured the Imam's base at Nizwa and drove the rebels up the Jebel Akhdar, which was the best such a small force could achieve.

In 1958 the British government agreed to provide assistance towards the reorganization of the Sultan's army, and in the early summer Colonel D. de C. Smiley, who had commanded the Blues, arrived in Muscat as Chief of Staff to the Sultan and in command of the Sultanas Armed Forces (SAF). He did not have many troops at his disposal: the Northern Frontier Regiment with 450 men was the backbone of the army, and the British component amounted to a troop of the 13/18th Hussars, with a brigade major and detachment of Royal Signals at headquarters. Periodically squadrons of the Trucial Oman Scouts were available.

It did not take Smiley long to appreciate that this small force was totally inadequate to dislodge the powerful band of rebels from their seemingly-impregnable mountain refuge, unconquered since remote antiquity. Moreover, they were not sitting placidly on the mountain plateau, but were causing serious vehicle and personnel casualties by the mining of roads and tracks. The Royal Air Force from Aden gave assistance with Shackleton bombers and Venom fighters (for at that time the Sultan's air force had just two single-engined machines), but bombing and strafing alone would not be sufficient. More British troops were needed. Smiley asked for two battalions, of which one should be a Royal Marine Commando, a Parachute battalion, or an SAS squadron. He was eventually given D Squadron of the Life Guards and D Squadron SAS.

JUNGLE TO MOUNTAIN

In October 1958 Lieutenant Colonel Anthony Deane-Drummond was in command of 22 SAS and, having confirmed from a quick reconnaissance in Oman that this was SAS work, he had been given fifteen days in which to extract D Squadron from the jungles of the Malaya/Thailand border and transport them to Oman. Somehow, by helicopter, marches, and rafts, the Squadron covered the 250 miles back to Kuala Lumpur in forty-eight hours. There then followed an intensive programme of training and reorganizing. In the jungle

Calibre: 7.62 mm	
Muzzle velocity: 2,750 ft/s	
Rate of fire: 30-40 rpm (single shot) or 650-700 rpm	
Weight: 11 lbs	
Magazine: 20 round box	

ILLUSTRATION BY: JON WILKINSON

FN (FABRIQUE NATIONALE) RIFLE

snap shooting at fleeting targets with sawn-off shotguns or FN (*Fabrique Nationale*) rifles was the formula, and a fight lasted only minutes. In desert conditions, with target visibility often up to 2,000 yards, it could last hours or days, and 3 inch mortars, rocket launchers, energa grenades (ballistic grenades fired from a rifle) and Brens would be needed.

The highest peaks of the Jebel Akhdar rise to over 8,000 feet, and at 6,000 feet there is a broad and fertile plateau 20 miles by 10, on which there are villages whose houses and crops then accommodated and fed the 600 or so rebels. There are also caves where they could shelter during air strikes. The steep approaches through narrow ravines were easily guarded, although some were considered by the rebels to be impassable. Daylight movement on the side of the mountain was impossible, for the enemy were alert, well armed with modern weapons and extremely good shots.

D Squadron, under Major Watts, arrived on 18 November, and four days later they commenced their first patrolling and probing. It was to be seven weeks before they could rest from their labours. Shortly before their arrival a patrol of the Muscat Regiment, led by Major Tony Hart, had discovered an unguarded route to the plateau, and while two SAS troops led by Captain Walker carried out fighting patrols on the southern side of the mountain – during which they lost a good corporal from a sniper's bullet – the other two accompanied Hart for a lodgement on the plateau. Walker and his men gained the plateau undiscovered, but came under attack from rebel strongpoints near a feature known as the Aqbat al Dhafar. The enemy although mauled could not be defeated, and the troops occupied sangar positions on the plateau, from which they operated patrols during December.

Meanwhile, on the south side of the Jebel in the Tanufarea the Life Guards (fighting stoutly in an unaccustomed infantry role) together with the Northern Frontier Regiment had a fierce battle, and the SAS troops, supported in the air

'...the SAS troops, supported in the air by Venoms, attacked a cave and killed a number of rebels.'

by Venoms, attacked a cave and killed a number of rebels. Life on the Jebel was extremely tough, with freezing temperatures and a bitterly cold wind by night, and the men pinned down by snipers in the hot daylight hours. Supply was by parachute, and not always reliable. On 27 December Walker's two troops carried out a strong night attack on the Aqbat position, with covering fire provided by the Life Guards. Having scaled the steep cliffs with ropes they engaged the rebels in hand-to-hand grapple inflicting casualties, but failing to break the fortitude and furious resolve of the embattled tribesmen.

Smiley, who was in overall command of all the troops, clearly saw the need for another SAS squadron, with which Deane-Drummond readily agreed. On 12 January Major Cooper's A Squadron arrived from Malaya, and it was not long before they were sent to relieve D Squadron, whose men were in need of a short rest – and incidentally of new boots, for the sharp rocks of the Jebel had played havoc with their special SAS ones.

Colonels Smiley and Deane-Drummond made many low flights over the Jebel, and from what they saw prepared their plan for the final eviction of the rebels. Like all good plans it was a simple one, based mainly on surprise through diversion and deception. In broad outline there was to be a feint

The de Havilland Venom fighter, the air support aircraft for the SAS.

A patrol moving out against insurgents.

(VIA IAN GARDINER AUTHOR OF IN SERVICE OF THE SULTAN.)

against the Aqbat al Dhafar which the enemy, expecting the attack to be made there, had reinforced. The main attack would go in from the Wadi Kamah, in the south, against the rebel strongholds in the Habib-Sharaijah area. Deane-Drummond had selected a likely-looking slope leading out of the wadi, which the pack animals could ascend even though there was no track.

This latter was important, for if the weather in the morning prevented flying the recently-imported Somaliland donkeys were the only means of resupply. On the night before the assault the head donkey wallahs were told in strictest confidence, with dire penalties for disclosure, that they were to lead their donkeys the next night up the Tanuf track – some 6 or 7 miles from the selected approach. It was learnt later that within twelve hours the rebels had this information. The poor little desert donkeys were to find the unaccustomed steep slope altogether too much for them, but their part in the deception, and the need to replace their loads by a parachute drop, contributed greatly to the success of the operation.

The feint against the Aqbat position was successful after two hours' close-quarters fighting, and A Squadron, less one troop, then made a forced march over very difficult country to join D ready for the attack on the night of 26 January. The march started at 8.30 p.m. with the SAS squadrons leading a troop of the Life Guards. The deception had been complete: only one picket remained to guard the chosen route, and this post was easily winkled out. The climb was extremely stiff, and to ensure that the plateau was reached before first light the leading troops dropped their bergens and scrambled up with only their rifles. But there was no resistance; the enemy had been outwitted. When they saw the resupply parachutes descending they mistook

'The situation developed into a colonial-type war, fought vicariously by Egypt and Russia on the one side and Britain and the Arab monarchies on the other.'

the canisters for men, and made the best haste they could to disappear. The arsenal they left to be captured was well stocked with most forms of modem weapons. The SAS lost two men when unluckily a sniper's bullet hit an energa grenade in one of the men's packs.

The next time that SAS troops were operational in South Arabia was in April 1964, following the declaration of an emergency by the Federal government (in 1963 Aden had joined the Federation of South Arabia, which included several of the British-protected tribal states in the hinterland of Aden) in December 1963.

Briefly, one of the immediate causes of trouble was the Egyptian-inspired revolt in the Yemen in September 1962, which overthrew the hereditary Imam and replaced him with a Republican regime that Britain did not recognize. There had for a long time been Yemeni claims to the Aden Protectorate and to Aden itself, and there was a strong pro-Yemeni faction in Aden led by the head of the trade unions. A year later, in December 1963, there was a bomb attack against the High Commissioner and Federal ministers at Aden airport, whereupon the Federal government closed the frontier with Yemen and declared a state of emergency.

The insurgency pot was well stirred by Nasser with his venomous and tendentious radio propaganda, and Russia wasted no time in backing Egypt, which sent a formidable army into the Yemen. The situation developed into a colonial-type war, fought vicariously by Egypt and Russia on the one side and Britain and the Arab monarchies on the other. A number of retired British soldiers, including Colonel Smiley and some ex-SAS men, took service as mercenaries with the Royalist Yemeni army under the Imam (who had escaped assassination), and fought with distinction over a period of almost eight years until at last, in 1969, a compromise peace was arranged by Saudi Arabia's King Faisal. But that was in the future; in 1964 the British and the Federation found themselves engaged in two very different types of campaign – a tribal uprising in the Radfan mountains of the Aden Protectorate, and urban guerrilla acts of terrorism in Aden State.

The five principal Radfan tribes could probably muster about 6,000 fighting men, all of them fine shots and good guerrilla potential. They were people who had lived very backward lives in great poverty, and they were therefore extremely susceptible to Egyptian promises of gold, weapons and ammunition in return for causing the maximum inconvenience to the Federation, and through it to the British. They started to cause trouble on the flimsy pretext that their lucrative customs trade – levied on caravans passing through their territory – had been stopped, and the Federation decided to take military action to uphold law and order. Accordingly an operation was launched at the beginning of January 1964 using three battalions of the Federal Regular Army, a troop of the 16/5th Lancers and some Gunners and Sappers. The operation was merely a demonstration in force to drive out a number of dissidents and show the tribesmen that the Federal government had the ability to enter the Radfan. It was entirely successful, but it merely sparked off more trouble with the Egyptian-backed Yemeni Republic, which stepped up its propaganda and actively encouraged rebellion. It was therefore decided to launch another, larger operation; and the Federation, under the terms of the Defence Treaty, requested the help of British troops.

A strong force of brigade strength, called Radforce, supported by the RAF, was to operate against the Radfan tribes to reassert authority and to stop various aggressive incidents. An intended short, sharp lesson that was to last about three weeks in fact stretched to three months before it was successfully concluded.

The SAS was only concerned in a small part of it. Its A Squadron was due to carry out training in the Aden area – between Borneo tours – during May and June 1964, and the commander. Major de la Billière, who was there making preparations, suggested bringing the Squadron over early in order to take part in the operation. This was agreed, and the Squadron – together with elements of Headquarters to make it self-supporting – flew from England in time for the planned brigade operation against some three to four thousand dissident tribesmen. By the time the Squadron arrived at Thumier in the Radfan mountains preliminary positions round the valley had already been taken up by infantry and Commando battalions, and the Squadron's pre-attack acclimatization took the form of long-distance patrols by night on the flanks of the infantry positions.

The plan was for Radforce to seize certain areas and tactical features so as to break up rebel strongholds. This was to be done through the capture of the prominent feature codenamed Cap Badge, and another known as Rice Bowl in the western half of the valley. There were to be four phases, and in phase three 22 SAS was to mark out a dropping zone for the 3rd Parachute Battalion on the night of 30 April/1 May. The task was given to a patrol of nine men under Captain Robin Edwards, and as they had a very long approach march up a wadi before reaching the forward defence lines they set off in armoured cars. However, the terrain did not permit the vehicles to get very far, and the patrol dismounted early in the evening of 29 April with about 8 miles of very steep going still to cover on foot. It was hoped they would reach their objective before first light and lie concealed until nightfall. However, the pace was slowed by one man who was unwell, and the party was short of its objective at dawn; but they were fortunate in

'...in the constant sniping exchanges two men were hit, and towards the end of the day when the enemy attempted to close in, the troop signaller was killed.'

finding two caves, or cracks in the rock, with sangars piled in front, which as part of the scenery should not attract unwelcome attention. Edwards reckoned that the comparatively easy remaining 3 miles to the projected DZ could be covered quite quickly at dusk.

Lying up in enemy territory is a most unrelaxing pastime, especially when there is little or no protection from the scorching sun, and movement of any kind is fraught with danger. It was therefore particularly galling that having obeyed all the rules, and endured several hours of suspense in sweltering heat, the patrol should have been discovered by the unlucky chance of a passing herdsman, who raised the alarm. In next to no time tribesmen were in action, and soon the patrol was surrounded at pretty close quarters. Edwards requested air support, and a close wireless link, via Squadron Headquarters, with the Brigade Air Support Officer ensured almost continuous strafing by Hunter aircraft throughout the day. This kept enemy heads down to a great extent; nevertheless in the constant sniping exchanges two men were hit, and towards the end of the day when the enemy attempted to close in, the troop signaller was killed.

Towards evening a heat haze put an end to air support, and Edwards had an urgent wireless conversation with the commander of 22 SAS (Lt-Colonel Michael Wingate-Gray) who was at Squadron Headquarters. With two men wounded and a shortage of ammunition and water there was now no chance of completing the mission, and Wingate-Gray ordered Edwards to break out. It was a near-hopeless situation in the face of tremendous odds, but it was achieved with considerable skill, the tribesmen being kept at bay by accurate covering fire – the patrol had one Bren – but soon after leaving the sangars Edwards was killed. Throughout the night the party, obviously tired and dispirited, wound their way over extremely rough and difficult going – a great ordeal for one man, badly wounded in the leg. An artillery stonk had discouraged pursuit, but three or four tribesmen caught up with the party, only to be expertly dealt with through a hastily-improvised ambush. An hour or two after first light on 1 May the seven survivors eventually reached safety.

A second attempt was made by another troop to mark out the DZ. But the enemy in that area were now fully alert, and the helicopters carrying the troop were badly shot up and forced to return. The parachute drop was then cancelled, and the Radforce plan adjusted accordingly.

There was a bizarre and unhappy sequel to this affair, when a propaganda broadcast from the Yemen announced that the heads of Captain Edwards and Trooper Warburton had been displayed on the walls of Sana – which was later confirmed through discovery of the decapitated bodies.

Not long afterwards A Squadron returned to England

as planned, but it and other squadrons would soon be back in the Federation carrying out very realistic training. The exemplary chastisement meted out in the Radfan campaign kept the rebel tribesmen from venturing anything on a large scale – until the British departure three years later, when they partook in the general upheaval to bring the Federation down - but they took every opportunity to carry out guerrilla warfare. Clashes were frequent and casualties quite high.

SAS patrols had a variety of tasks, laid down by Headquarters, Middle East, in both the Radfan and the Aden hinterland. These included the establishment of cleverly-concealed forward observation posts from which they could direct artillery fire and air strikes on parties of the enemy, and the interception of arms and supplies being sent to the Aden city revolutionaries. This latter involved long-distance patrolling, and ambushing routes from the North Yemen border. The extreme heat and shortage of water in the barren, ridge-backed Radfan mountains made this gruelling work, and some may have envied their colleagues the more arcane, although equally dangerous, duties in Aden State.

Terrorism had begun there in late 1963, shortly after the British government had announced their intention of pulling out not later than 1968. There was no longer much reason for the local Arabs to show any great loyalty to people who would soon be unable to protect them, and Egypt was not slow to point out the wisdom of hastening the departure of the 'oppressors'. The Egyptian-sponsored National Liberation Front proved a very successful terrorist organization, infiltrating its members into many influential posts from where they carried out acts of intimidation, assassination and some indiscriminate grenade throwing.

SAS – A VARIED ROLE

The SAS role was mainly an undercover one in the rat-ridden, adulterated alleys of Aden. From a central headquarters about twenty specially picked men, whose features most lent themselves to the impersonation of natives, would split into parties of two or three and infiltrate into districts of the Crater and Sheikh Othman, where the hard-core terrorists were most active. Military intelligence was important and very scarce, so even the occasional arrest and subsequent successful interrogation was of great value. SAS men occasionally brought off an important arrest, or outgunned some evilly-disposed thugs, but on the whole not very much was accomplished in this their first attempt at

The new Sultan, Said Qaboos.
(VIA IAN GARDINER AUTHOR OF *IN SERVICE OF THE SULTAN*.)

undercover operations; although lessons learnt in training and in action were to prove useful in the future.

The longest, most important and most fruitful work that the SAS was to do in South Arabia resulted from their presence throughout the Dhofar war, which lasted (as far as the SAS were concerned) from 1970 until 1976. The province of Dhofar lies at the south end of Oman, and is about the size of Wales. Its inhabitants are of different stock from the northern Arabs, and for the most part live a hard life on the Jebel massif, which runs parallel to the sea, forming a backdrop to the coastal plain which in some places, such as Salalah, is very narrow. The Jebel rises steeply behind the plain to form a plateau at some 3,000 ft. From June to September it is washed by the south-west monsoon (khareef), and the plateau is pleasantly lush. But as water becomes scarce in the dry months the Jebelis abandon their dwellings for the caves of the deep wadis that scar the mountain side. Water is the key to life on the Jebel, and the Jebel was at that time the key to life in Dhofar.

The regime of Sultan Said bin Taimur was medieval in concept and totally lacking in any form of progress. There was great poverty and much disease, no hospitals and no education – many sought this elsewhere, sometimes in Russia – and inhuman punishments were meted out for any transgression of the Sultan's word, which was law. And yet Said was not entirely bad; he was a well-educated, courteous but misguided man who thought to solve his country's problems by isolation and autocratic policies. Instead he sowed the seeds of rebellion, which first broke out, in a minor way, in 1962. The repressive punitive measures that followed only made matters worse, and the rebels formed a political party – the Dhofar Liberation Front, which later became the People's Front for the Liberation of the Arabian Gulf- which was quickly backed by the recently formed People's Democratic Republic of the Yemen (PDRY), by the Russians and, until 1972, by the Chinese.

From these and other sources the rebels received arms and financial support, and Oman was rapidly clattering into anarchy. Something had to be done to lift the Sultan's affairs out of the catalepsy by which they were afflicted, and the Sultan's son did just that by lifting the Sultan out of his palace in an almost bloodless *coup d'état* on 23 July 1970. The new Sultan, Qaboos, was then twenty-nine years of age, he had been educated at Sandhurst and had very different ideas from his father. He at once declared an amnesty, and launched plans for development in every department. The amnesty brought a number of the rebels, who had become fed up with Communist atrocities and ideology, back to their allegiance, but it had little effect on the many hardliners, and the PDRY doubled its efforts at coercion.

Sultan Qaboos realized, and so did the British commander of the Sultan's Armed Forces, that his troops were not sufficiently well equipped nor trained to drive the rebels from the Jebel and to occupy it permanently themselves. He therefore sought help from Britain and later from Iran, Jordan, India and Pakistan. The response was good, for it was in everyone's interest to ensure that Oman did not fall into the hands of an unfriendly power – but it was always understood that the war was the Sultanas and foreign troops acted only under his overall command while in Dhofar.

Military hardware of every kind was one requirement, but equally important was the need to win the 'hearts and minds' of thejebelis, and to improve the lot – medically, educationally and nutritionally – of the entire population. Lieutenant Colonel Watts, then commanding 22 SAS, was sent to Oman to make a report. The subsequent fulfilment of his recommendations has been brilliantly described by Colonel A S Jeaps in his book SAS: Operation *Oman*.

Civil and military aid could be only on a temporary basis with a view to bringing immediate relief while the Omanis themselves were being trained to take over. With this in mind Watts stressed the need for five immediate requirements, all of which the SAS with their varied skills were well able to give. They were medical assistance, intelligence gathering, information dissemination (not mindless propaganda, but the simple

> '**Military hardware of every kind was one requirement, but equally important was the need to win the 'hearts and minds' of the Jebelis**'

truth and only the truth), veterinary aid – for the Dhofaris placed great store on their live-stock – and the training of tribesmen willing to fight the rebels.

At first all that the SAS were permitted to send was a totally inadequate party of nineteen men, but in February 1971 the first full squadron arrived; thereafter throughout the war squadrons did, as in Borneo, four-monthly tours, and on one occasion Colonel Watts had two squadrons in Dhofar. The initial party, under Captain Shaw, which came into Dhofar under the official designation British Army Training Team (BATT), although small, rapidly made its presence felt. It included a medical and veterinary officer, and Shaw soon arranged for two four-man Civil Action Teams to set up clinics in Taqa and Mirbat, two towns on the coast east of Salalah.

These small Civil Action Teams were an extremely important feature of the SAS work in Dhofar. They always included a medic and at least one Arabic speaker; they travelled by Land-Rover and at each village they visited they immediately established a clinic, and did what they could for the large number of people suffering from every form of medical neglect. Their reports on the food and water conditions in the areas where the fighting had receded were of value to the government's Civil Aid Department (CAD), which would arrange food distribution, drill wells and improve educational facilities. There was a lot to be done (and even more in the early days before the CAD was set up), and the veterinary officer had an equally stern task, for the tribesmen's animals were, if anything, in a worse state than the tribesmen themselves.

The Landrover equipped the British forces, including the SAS, taking the place of the Jeep. (VIA IAN GARDINER AUTHOR OF *IN SERVICE OF THE SULTAN.*)

TRAINING THE FIRQATS

But the greatest contribution of the SAS to the Sultan's ultimate victory was their work with those fierce bands of paramilitary men which were known as the firqats. They were mostly made up from surrendered enemy who were carefully screened, given a short period to think things over and then invited to join their tribal firqat. They were a hard, wild, unpredictable lot wrought by a lifetime of fighting, but their knowledge of the ground, and the snowballing effect their successes had, made them an invaluable part of the SAP – even if they did not always see eye to eye with the Omani soldiers. Starting in a fairly humble way, their numbers grew almost weekly and by 1975 there were twenty-one firqats widely dispersed and totalling about 1,600 men. There was a headquarters for Firqat Forces, commanded by Lieutenant Colonel McLean, which had the difficult task of undertaking overall administration.

The Firqat Salahadin was the first to be raised by the SAS/BATT, under its bold, charismatic fugleman, Salim Mubarak. Discipline was always something of a problem and Salim Mubarak thought that it would be easier to enforce in a multi-tribal firqat, which would avoid the tribal passion for equality. But it did not prove a success and the system was not continued, all subsequent firqats being tribal. No virtue was more necessary than patience in trying to organize, train and equip these enthusiastic, temperamental tribesmen, and the small SAS teams in the difficult role of advisers, not commanders, did a magnificent job.

IN THE SERVICE OF THE SULTAN

Extracted from *In Service of the Sultan*
<u>By Ian Gardiner</u>

The word firqat means a military unit or group. The Firqat Forces units were made up of Dhofari Jebali tribesmen, many of who had been fighting on the other side but who had been persuaded to come over to the Sultan. These people were called Surrendered Enemy Personnel – SEPs – but it was a misnomer because it implied that they had been beaten. As soldiers, they were not beaten, but the political system which had recruited them was. Many of them had been trained by Russian or Chinese advisors.

Regular soldiers could find the firqat infuriating. The SAS, who themselves were somewhat irregular, and were trained to train irregular soldiers, were mostly pretty well adjusted to the task. However the firqat were a law unto themselves.

They were also expensive. They were supplied and paid like any other military formation. It was best not to be too rigorous with the arithmetic when counting them

Ian Gardiner amusing himself with a .50 Browning machine gun.

as there were always ghosts on the payroll and it was not easy to see what the Sultan was getting for his money. They were intensely tribal and would only work in their own particular tribal area and so, to the orderly military eye, they had limited utility. They had to believe in your ability to assist them, whether by rudimentary first aid,

A barefooted firqat soldier.

or by providing rations, ammunition, water, artillery or aircraft. Mike Kingscote became an expert at building roads, schools, mosques, houses and at sinking wells. He even found himself delivering a baby on one occasion.

Orders and firqat did not go well together. Everything required negotiation and time. Mike's negotiations with the firqat to participate in any specific operation tended to be lengthy and tortuous. Where was the operation? When do we leave? How many people do you want? How long are we going to be away? Reasonable enough questions perhaps, but often he suspected they were inspired by a wish to warn their 'cousins' that they were coming, or for some other agenda that he would never know. The trick was to keep the destination a secret for as long as possible, and then fly in rather than walk.

Mike Kingscote's description of one of the operations he conducted illustrates well the 'alternative' approach that the firqat had to fighting. He and his firqat were ambushing a water hole, supported by an Army company and an SAS detachment. They moved in and set up the ambush during the night. At dawn, Mike found he was on an exposed slope and in a complex of disused sangars. His sangar was overhung by a tree, but he had a good view of the water hole. He was armed with a machine gun.

As dawn broke, we scrutinised the area very carefully. While this was happening, I saw a member of the firqat behind me lighting solid fuel blocks underneath an enormous kettle in the bottom of the sangar. I was very surprised and suggested that it might be better if he were

> 'There was no question of; "how did it go?" or "are you all right?" Merely; "has the kettle boiled?"'

to concentrate on the purpose at hand. He smiled and handed me a packet of sweet biscuits. At the same time Ahmed Ali, with whom I was sharing the sangar, and I saw at least ten adoo, possibly more, moving about in our killing area. The order to open fire was given.

I rattled my way through a couple of magazines, and received an RPG 7 rocket round into the base of my sangar, which showered Ahmed and me with dust and gravel. We continued firing and the next RPG round hit the tree above our heads, this time showering us with metal and branches. The SAS team, seeing that we were attracting the weight of the adoo's fire, fired a rocket grenade into the enemy position and scored a direct hit. I was relieved, as having been bracketed with two rounds, I knew where the next one was going.

In the brief respite that followed, Ahmed Ali and I reloaded as fast as we could. I noticed that we were alone in the sangar. The other firqat members had disappeared. I asked Ahmed where they were. He said, *'over the hill'*. As the RPG rockets had started coming in, they had disappeared in the opposite direction. The firefight continued for another ten or fifteen minutes, and then the Army company started to move in from a flank. It was at this stage, the firqat members started to emerge. There was no question of; *'how did it go?'* or *'are you all right?'* Merely; *'has the kettle boiled?'*

Thereafter he resolved to keep the firqat in front of him so that he could see what they were doing.

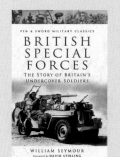
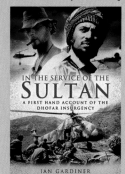

THE SAS IN RECENT TIMES

Between the ending of the Dhofar campaign in 1976 and the Falklands battle in 1982 there was no war in which the SAS took part. But over the years as their fame spread there was, and still is, an increasing demand for their services in many parts of the world, and in various roles.

By William Seymour

Extracted from *British Special Forces* and reproduced by permission of Pen & Sword Books Ltd.

Men have been loaned to heads of state for such purposes as training of bodyguards, and in at least one case – Oman – raising and training whole SAS-type units. Small parties are sent unobtrusively to survey possible trouble spots, where military action might be required; instructors are provided for the Long Range Patrol School in Germany, which is connected to NATO; at home there is the need for constant readiness in the very important anti-terrorist role, and since 1976 there has been the Irish commitment on a regular basis.

The SAS understandably shun publicity and, until some eye-catching event such as the Iranian Embassy siege hits the headlines, little is heard of their present-day activities – and that is how they like it. But where the dictates of secrecy do not intrude there is a natural desire to know something about Britain's foremost special service, what they have done and what they are training

to do. And this mostly concerns 22 SAS based on Stirling Lines, Hereford.

22 SAS has four 'Sabre' squadrons. A, B, D and G. The missing C was the Rhodesian squadron formed at the time of the Malay Scouts, and which remained in being until that country became Zimbabwe. G Squadron was formed shortly after Borneo, as a Guards squadron, but now guardsmen usually comprise less than fifty per cent of the strength. Each squadron has a boat, mountain, free-fall and mobility troop – the latter are motorcycle experts and skilled in the mechanics of every

'The SAS understandably shun publicity and, until some eye-catching event such as the Iranian Embassy siege hits the headlines, little is heard of their present-day activities.'

type of potential enemy vehicle. A troop is commanded by a captain and there are fifteen other ranks.

Basically the four squadrons rotate between Northern Ireland, Special Project Teams, overseas training, standby, skills training and leave. The standby squadron, which is available to fly anywhere for a military job, can be on training in this country or abroad as long as it has with it the necessary kit for an emergency deployment elsewhere. The Special Project Teams (formerly known as Pagoda) can vary in strength, but are found from one squadron, and one team will always be on immediate call and a second at three hours' notice. There is also a team permanently in Ireland with reinforcements on call from Hereford. In order to achieve the very highest standard of excellence in quick shooting and close-quarters combat, so essential for survival and success in any anti-terrorist operation, a Counter-Revolutionary Wing (CRW) was set up some years ago, whose importance has been increasingly recognized with a consequent considerable improvement in its training facilities and weaponry. The CRW has a staff of some twenty men (usually a three-year job) fulfilling a wide variety of training tasks, of which the principal one is the running of the Body Guard (BG) and Close Quarter Battle (CQB) courses. These involve hard work in the indoor CQB building – colloquially known as 'the House', an abbreviation from 'the Killing House'. On these courses every man is provided with a minimum of 1,500 rounds of ammunition and taught, among other things, to handle a wide assortment of weapons with a deadly familiarity, and to deal most expeditiously with magazine changes and possible stoppages,

'The House' is realistically furnished to resemble an ordinary (but bullet-proof) sitting-room with terrorists

> 'On first bursting into the room the man must be able to distinguish hostage from terrorist, and then carry out fire and movement of exceptional accuracy and velocity.'

and hostages represented by dummies. Training is carried out with the many sophisticated weapons now used, such as the Heckler and Koch MP5 9 mm submachine gun; the American-made Ingram machine pistol; the Browning automatic 13-round pistol; stun grenades; and tear gas. On first bursting into the room the man must be able to distinguish hostage from terrorist, and then carry out fire and movement of exceptional accuracy and velocity, not to spray the room but to thump a couple of bullets into an enemy before he can even bring his weapon to the ready. Obviously surprise is an essential ingredient in this type of fighting – as in most types – and is often obtained by gas and grenades. But the reflex action required for this quick, close-quarters killing business against alert, well-armed thugs holed up in a small space has to be even more strongly developed than that needed for the equally dangerous street fighting.

The CRW staff, as well as running the BG and CQB courses, are closely concerned with the training of the Special Project Teams. When, for example, a squadron returns from training abroad and is due to take up the SP role, the handing-over squadron may run a refresher course for the newcomers, but the CRW are on hand to co-ordinate the training and teach the various specialist skills, such as observation-post work. It is understandable, therefore, that the CRW and the Special Project Teams need to spend very many hours in 'the House'; but the building can be booked by any troop at Hereford which wishes to brush up its close-combat skills. Every man in 22 SAS has to be fully trained for this work.

There are numerous civil and political threads to be unravelled before a Special Project Team of the SAS goes

HECKLER & KOCH MP5 SUBMACHINE GUN

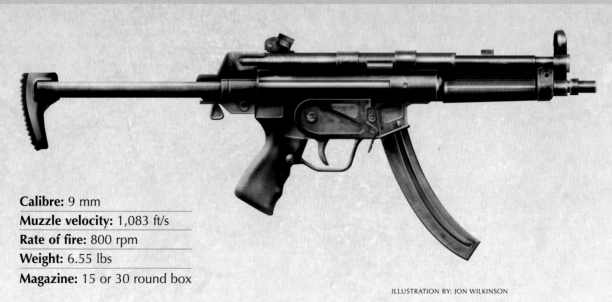

Calibre: 9 mm
Muzzle velocity: 1,083 ft/s
Rate of fire: 800 rpm
Weight: 6.55 lbs
Magazine: 15 or 30 round box

ILLUSTRATION BY: JON WILKINSON

into action. The police, at any rate initially, will handle acts of criminal intimidation and violence, and when political terrorism is involved the committee known as COBRA (Cabinet Office Briefing Room), which is chaired by the Deputy Prime Minister, directs the operation. The SAS are represented by advisers on this body and are therefore in direct touch. Negotiations and persuasion are tried exhaustively by the police, sometimes with success. But on other occasions impossible demands are relayed back to COBRA and are dealt with patiently and diplomatically, while preparations for a possible break-in proceed quietly on the spot. Then, perhaps, the terrorists' patience runs out and a hostage is murdered. Such deeds sow their crop of dragons' teeth, and when this happens terrorists can expect no mercy, for then a Special Project Team will surely be unleashed.

IRANIAN EMBASSY SIEGE

The classic example of this is, of course, the Iranian Embassy siege, when on the morning of 30 April 1980 six Arab nationalists forced their way into that embassy – taking with them in the process the police constable on guard – and for five-and-a-half days held some twenty-one hostages (including four women) captive, until on the evening of 5 May they brutally murdered the Iranian press attaché and threatened, unless their demands were met, to perpetrate similar acts of violence every half hour.

The SAS team were on site a few hours after the trouble had started. They travelled from Hereford in plain clothes, and took up temporary quarters in a truck at Hyde Park Corner. During the long days of tedious and futile negotiation they assisted, from the neighbouring house, in making tiny peepholes through the adjoining walls by which a fish-eye television camera could record the exact layout and position of hostages and terrorists. Then, on the evening of the fifth day, when the head of the Metropolitan Police on the spot reported the assassination to COBRA, the decision was made by the Prime Minister, Mrs Thatcher, to send in the SAS.

The thrilling and extremely successful twelve-minute attack that followed has been often and fully described; within less than forty-five minutes the building had been cleared of terrorists, all but one of whom had been killed, the hostages – save the assistant press attaché, who was of course already dead – had been rescued unharmed, and the SAS had handed the building back to the police.

The five principal ingredients for the success of this operation were first and foremost the high standard of professionalism of those taking part, born of many months' careful preparation and training in 'the House'. Secondly, there was the use made of the time allowed for reconnaissance; the photographs of the gunmen, armed with their formidable Uzi submachine guns, and of the occupied rooms, indicating the type of opposition to be encountered and the probable location of hostages. Thirdly, men had been able to spend time on the roof

making preparations for the difficult abseiling manoeuvres to blast their way into the back and front of the building. Fourthly, the choice of weapons proved exactly right for the task – framed charges of plastic explosive, stun grenades, CS gas, personal intercommunication wireless, and the deadly machine pistols so expertly handled. And fifthly – among the twenty-five SAS men engaged there was at least one with knowledge of Arabic and Farsi.

OTHER OPERATIONS

There have been other less spectacular but fairly similar operations carried out by small SAS teams, and no doubt more that have never been disclosed, for the Regiment has worldwide anti-terrorist interests in an advisory, exploratory, protective and reconnaissance capacity. In January 1975 the hijacking of an aeroplane from Manchester ended in farce when the hijacker, an Iranian with a dummy pistol, found an SAS reception party awaiting him at Stansted airport, where he was landed – much to his surprise – instead of the hoped-for Paris. And later that year in London four members of the IRA, trapped by the police in a Balcombe Street flat, decided to give themselves up when they learned that the SAS were preparing to come in and get them. But the Lufthansa hijack from Malta in October 1977, in which two SAS men (Major Morrison and Sergeant Davies) played a prominent part, was a much more serious business. The hijack was carried out by four Palestinian terrorists, who were demanding the return by the West German government of certain members of the Baader-Meinhof gang – and there were no dummy pistols in their armoury. After the Munich massacre in 1972 the Germans had raised their own anti-terrorist squad (GSG-9), and when the hijacked aircraft was known to be heading for Dubai – a state which had close British affiliations – a senior member of GSG-9 flew to London to seek help. As SAS men had trained the Dubai Royal Guard and knew the area, the offer of their services was gratefully accepted. In the event the airliner left Dubai before action could be taken and flew on to Aden, where the aircraft carrying GSG-9 and SAS was refused permission to land. Eventually both aeroplanes landed at Mogadishu, where the terrorists flung on to the tarmac the body of the pilot whom they had murdered. Until then the Germans were fully prepared to negotiate - they had £9 million on board – but as in London three years later murder sealed the fate of the terrorists.

By now the GSG-9 backup force had arrived and the plan, a bold one, was quickly worked out by the SAS team and the Germans. The two SAS men were to fling their percussion grenades from each side of the aircraft, and this was to be the signal for the immediate assault by the Germans, who would bash in the emergency doors above the wings. The entry into the airliner went according to plan, and there ensued an eight-minute gun battle against terrorists in the front and rear of the machine; bullets hummed over the heads of the seventy-nine passengers still strapped in their seats, who suffered no worse fate than the harmless explosion of two terrorist grenades beneath their seats, while the quick-shooting Germans killed three of the four terrorists and made fast the fourth. This fruitful piece of international co-operation enhanced the reputation of both special forces.

Contrary to what is sometimes thought, and indeed to what has appeared in print, neither the SAS, nor any individual member of it, had any commitment whatever in Northern Ireland before the then Prime Minister, Harold Wilson, announced in January 1976 that a squadron was to be sent, in a combatant role, to the troublesome and virtually uncontrolled border area of South Armagh. The only previous visit had been when a squadron was sent to Northern Ireland for ten days to practise emergency deployment. Their absence until 1976 was in some part due to the heavy commitments they had at the time elsewhere, principally South Arabia – and the fact that propaganda put out by the IRA had effectively stopped their use, because politicians had previously denied their presence, even though no one believed that.

When they were sent to the Province it was in the normal role being carried out by other regiments there, in other words surveillance, patrols, ambushes and so on; at no time did they engage in undercover work, nor did they work with the 'counter-gang' Military Reconnaissance Force, known as 'Freds', nor at any time with Military Intelligence – which later was perhaps a pity, for during the early 1970s the whole intelligence network in Northern Ireland was shrouded in Cimmerian gloom and general confusion, with MIS and MI6 in close competition and rivalry. As the Dhofar campaign had only recently been concluded at the time of the Prime Minister's statement, it was a little while before a full squadron could be assembled in the Crossmaglen area, but an advance party was early on the scene and very soon satisfactory results were achieved in that dark district. Only the more sensational actions reach the newspapers, and many successes by British soldiers and the police – often bloodless – in the field of ambuscade, finding of arms caches and co-operation with the Royal Ulster Constabulary frequently occur, but are seldom reported.

The SAS skills in well-concealed observation work, perhaps extending for long periods, the speedy transmission of vital intelligence, fast and accurate shooting, and the siting of ambushes soon won for them both respect and obloquy from the IRA.

Confusion and calumny have occasionally caused them to suffer adverse publicity. As a declared force they have sometimes been used as the stalking horse for other highly-secretive operatives; on other occasions they have been blatantly accused of atrocities that never occurred; and of course at times there have been mistakes which might perhaps have been avoided. When such mistakes do occur – and it is seldom enough – they usually stem from the very difficult position in which every soldier finds himself while serving in Northern Ireland. He is at one and the same time acting in aid of the civil power and fighting an undeclared war; a whole mishmash of hand-tying rules and regulations bind him which, when violated or disregarded in the slightest degree, are immediately seized upon by his opponents, who in their turn recognize no law but their own caprice.

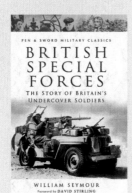
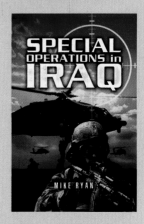

5.56mm, M16 rounds or a grenade splinter - breached the fuel tank of an aircraft, releasing fuel onto the grass. Another something, perhaps a tracer round, parachute flare, LAW rocket or 40mm grenade fragment, ignited the petrol soaking into the grass strip..'

THE RAID ON PEBBLE ISLAND

HMS *Glamorgan*'s log for 15 May 1982 indicates, '0400 hrs Arrived on the gun-line ... 0420 hrs Opened fire and 0745 hrs Bombardment complete. Retired at 29 knots! 14 Aircraft destroyed ashore'. Between those times, and beyond the bare bones of these facts, much had happened on Pebble Island.

By Francis MacKay with Jon Cooksey

This article was extracted from *Pebble Island - The Falklands War 1982* and is reproduced here by permission of Pen and Sword Books Ltd.

Glamorgan left the Task Group at 2000 hrs; followed by *Hermes* and *Broadsword* at 2030 hrs. As Air Surveillance and Defence ship (albeit with the elderly 35-mile range Sea Slug SAM) *Glamorgan* preceded *Hermes*. *Broadsword* acted as the anti-submarine escort and point anti-aircraft defence ship (with the short-range, vertical launch Sea Wolf system) on the main air threat flank and at some distance away from the other ships' wakes to improve sonar reception. The ships skirted the northern edge of the enemy radar envelope. Fortunately the Argentinians' last Neptune had just been struck off strength, depriving them of long-range radar-surveillance aircraft at just the wrong time.

The wind had increased during the day and by evening was again gusting Force Seven, with accompanying sea states. During the transit to fly-off position the weather created problems for *Hermes*' aircraft-handlers when the Sea Kings were brought up onto the flightdeck from the hangar; problems compounded by a faulty lift mechanism. The weather also forced the Navigating Officer, the Air Planning staff and the helicopter pilots to re-calculate ship and helicopter transit times and fuel consumption. That meant *Hermes* would have to move further west to launch and recover the helicopters twice – a decidedly dangerous situation, given the probable air and submarine threat.

Lieutenant Commander Roger Edwards remarked that;

'When we eventually boarded for the mission the aircraft we used had been on deck for a considerable period as we had boarded them once and then had to disembark while Hermes steamed flat out to within range of Pebble Island.

> 'Despite careful route-planning, the ships were plotted by the Argentinians in Stanley and were reported as moving within the radar shadow.'

These aircraft would have remained on deck for the six hours or so until the ship was within range. We went below to the Aircrew Ready Room and spent the time drinking coffee and having a smoke.'

At that point, *Broadsword*'s Sea Wolf system broke-down. Due to the sea-state the ship had to reduce speed to allow the trainable missile launcher to be locked and disarmed before repairs could take place. That, coupled with strong headwinds, made her fall behind the other ships, causing *Hermes* to slow to ensure she was covered by *Broadsword*'s weapon systems. *Glamorgan* therefore also slowed to keep all three vessels within the Sea Slug engagement zone. Once repairs had been completed the ships headed west at high speed.

Despite careful route-planning, the ships were plotted by the Argentinians in Stanley and were reported as

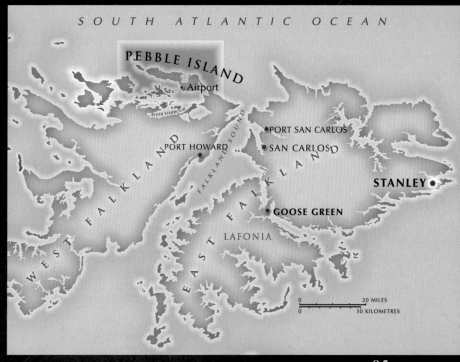

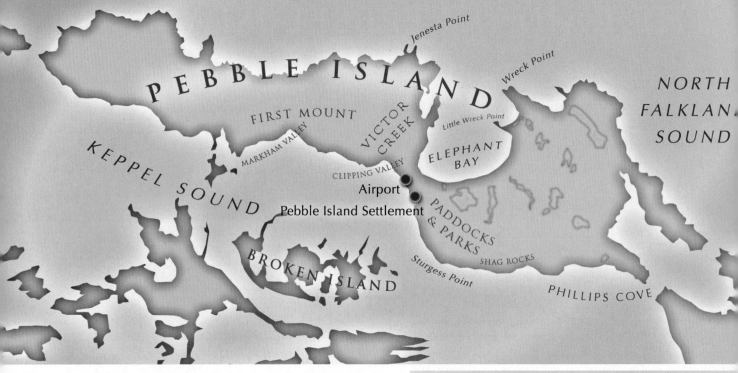

PEBBLE ISLAND

Jenesta Point

Wreck Point

NORTH
FALKLAND
SOUND

FIRST MOUNT

VICTOR
CREEK

Little Wreck Point

MARKHAM VALLEY

ELEPHANT
BAY

KEPPEL SOUND

CLIPPING VALLEY

Airport

Pebble Island Settlement

PADDOCKS
& PARKS

SHAG ROCKS

BROKEN ISLAND

Sturgess Point

PHILLIPS COVE

moving within the radar shadow. Stanley alerted Lieutenant Marega to the reappearance of three ships heading west past the northern coast of Pebble Island. The Argentinian GHQ may have assessed these movements over the previous two nights to be associated with the radar picket north of the island.

At 0200 hrs *Hermes* reduced speed and launched the Sea Kings twenty-five minutes later and by a variety of signal routes, that information was passed to Boat Troop on Pebble Island. The carrier and *Broadsword* retired to loiter outside the radar envelope, ready to return to recover the helicopters for refuelling for the recovery sortie.

On *Glamorgan,* Major Eve made final adjustments to maps and the Fireplan prepared for the ship's Operations Centre staff. He also had a final word with Lieutenant Commander Inskip. During one of the planning sessions a discrepancy of 400 yards was found between naval charts and land maps due to changes of grid origin; once that had been detected and allowed for the first naval gunfire support salvo onto Borbon (the Argentinean garrison on Pebble Island) was to prove remarkable.

Glamorgan closed to her designated Fire Support

HMS Glamorgan *showing 4.5 inch gun turret.*

HMS Hermes.

HMS Broadsword *dipping bows into heavy sea.*

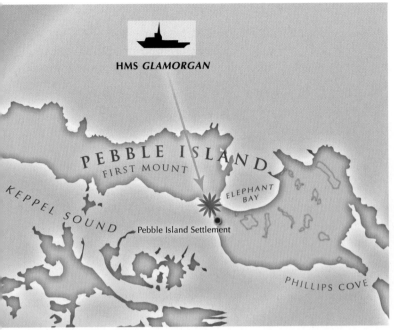

HMS *GLAMORGAN*

HMS GLAMORGAN'S DESIGNATED FIRE SUPPORT AREA

Area, slightly north-west of, and some six miles from, Borbon to allow for the strong westerly wind and provide maximum burn-time for Star Shell flares which are ignited and ejected at the top of the shell's trajectory.

After the Sea Kings left the immediate area of *Hermes* they descended to low level and headed for the east end of Pebble Island. Roger Edwards again:

'The weather generally was very cold and foggy for that time of year and did cause some problems landing folks ashore. On the night of the raid it was generally good visibility but with a gale from the WNW. I can remember quite a large sea running as every now and again a breaking crest could be seen level with the door of the Sea King – we were quite low!'

Meanwhile, on Pebble Island, Boat Troop, less a two-man observation post watching the approaches from the airfield and settlement, had re-assembled at Phillips Cove. While his men enjoyed a quick brew, made for them by the landing site guards, Captain Burls briefed those not keeping watch on what had been seen of Borbon and on the routes and obstacles. He then allocated tasks. First was nomination, or rather confirmation, of the helicopter marshalling team. He confirmed that the evacuation landing zone would be close to the mortar base plate position. The Sea Kings would fly to the Cove and then hug the ridge-crests looking for the marshal's torches.

Secondly, guides were appointed for the various assault groups and the position of the mortar base-plate position briefed and located on maps. Reinforcements were sent to the OP by the settlement, carrying as much ammunition as could be spared for GPMGs, to disrupt any attempt at interference if the helicopters were detected on their way in to the cove.

Captain Burls prepared to brief the incoming Squadron but they were later than expected.

The helicopters arrived at 0350 hrs, homing in on the marshal's torches in turn and hovering, wheels barely touching the ground, to unload the heavily laden raiding party. 'We landed facing North,' recalled Roger Edwards, ' on the left of the valley so that on exit we went downhill away from the rotors.' A brief message announcing safe arrival was passed up the chain of command. The helicopters returned to *Hermes* to refuel and, as time was so short, to start the evacuation. There was never any question of waiting on the carrier for a recovery call.

On *Glamorgan* Major Eve and his navy signaller, Leading Radio Operator Wilcox, had everything ready. The naval gunfire support part of the Fire Plan, code-named *Antarctic Fox*, could be initiated whenever it was needed; the guns were ready to be loaded with the first rounds (Star-shell), and all targets were plotted, and checked. After sorting out a slight confusion over radio frequencies and learning of the successful insertion of the raiding party, Major Eve opened up on the naval gunfire officer's (NGFO) radio net at 0400 hrs, informing Captain Brown that *Glamorgan* was on the Gun-line.

In reply Captain Brown - NGFO5 - advised him that naval gunfire would not be required until 0630 hrs due to the delay in landing. However, as there were now friendly forces ashore who might require it at any time, and as the ship was in hostile waters, *Glamorgan* stood to Action Stations. Major Eve stood ready to receive situation reports or calls for illumination or fire support.

Sea Kings loading the raiding party aboard HMS **Hermes***.*

*An SAS soldier armed with
the M16 assault rifle fitted
with an M203 grenade
launcher. Most of the
troopers carried an M16 or
a General Purpose Machine
Gun and at least one LAW
66. Little webbing was
worn so as not to inhibit
mobility during the raid.*
ILLUSTRATION BY JON WILKINSON

It was now 0415 hrs, just over three hours before sunrise. H-Hour, the time the assault force would cross the start-line, had been set for 0630 hrs, so the raiders had to reach their targets, mount the attack and return very quickly indeed. It should be remembered that many men of D Squadron had been in action under severe weather conditions on South Georgia, and had then lived in some discomfort on board ship. It is also worth bearing in mind that such a large raid, even on exercise, was a very unusual, if not unique event, for an entire modern-day SAS Squadron to undertake.

At Phillips Cove the incoming troops rapidly cleared the immediate area of the LZ and clustered at the top of the valley above the Cove, covered by Boat Troop's sentries. Captain Burls quickly updated

'It is also worth bearing in mind that such a large raid, even on exercise, was a very unusual, if not unique event, for an entire modern-day SAS Squadron to undertake.'

Major Delves, WOII Gallagher and the troop leaders. He, in turn, was briefed by his commanding officer. The plan of attack was rapidly reviewed so that everyone was up to speed with information gathered by Boat Troop.

The plan, essentially, followed the outline set on *Hermes*, with one change. Boat Troop – whose task was to act as guides and provide the covering party for the settlement - would also be the rearguard during the withdrawal. Mountain Troop was to cover the mortar position and evacuation landing zone, while Mobility Troop was to be the airfield assault force. The change was that Air Troop, plus RNLO, would not now assault the settlement but provide a barrier between it and the airfield. HQ and Captain Brown would be in what had been designated as the Fire Support Base, forward of the mortar position, close to the barrier and able to observe the airfield area. The Start Line for the airfield assault would be a fence running between the pond near Elephant Beach to the settlement. The withdrawal rendezvous would be at the mortar base plate position.

Around that time (0410 hrs) *Glamorgan*'s Principal Weapons Officer advised Artillery Liason that, as the visibility was good, the ship would have to come off the Gun Line at 0730 hrs, (shortly after sunrise at 0728 hrs) and depart the Fire Support Area to gain the safety of the British air patrol umbrella, some thirty miles away, by daylight. Captain Brown requested the ship be ready to fire the first rounds at 0700 hrs. Artillery Liason acknowledged, indicating that *Glamorgan* was ready to execute Fireplan *Antarctic Fox*.

approach march. During the night Major Delves had revised the timetable to allow for the various delays. Here he threw caution to the wind but it was a calculated risk. Instead of the Troops and HQ group taking separate routes, everyone would head for the settlement at high speed and in single file, himself in front with Captain Burls as guide. The order of march would be; HQ group; mortar team; Air Troop; remainder of Boat Troop; Mountain Troop; Mobility Troop.

The Squadron took off, led by Captain Burls, compass in hand and counting paces, moving quickly despite their heavy loads. A rising westerly wind scattered the light cloud cover, providing intermittent light from the moon, in its last quarter. *'There was good visibility'*, according to Roger Edwards, *'First Mountain could be seen as a big black shape ahead of us.'*

At 0610 hrs the mortar base plate position was

took off, led by Captain Burls, compass in hand and counting paces, moving quickly despite their heavy loads.'

started to set-up the weapon. As the other raiders passed, each dropped their bomb-carriers in a pile. The base-plate was dropped, the barrel fitted, the bipod erected, sights clipped in place and the sighting-post set-up; the mortar was ready to fire by 0615 hrs. While the mortarman checked the sights his colleagues stacked the bomb-carriers in two piles, parachute illumination and HE, unscrewing the caps of each tube to expose the rounds, ready for quick withdrawal.

The HQ Group and Air Troop reached their position by the slope leading down to the settlement, where Air Troop sited GPMGs to cover the settlement and the surrounding slopes. They were in luck. The wind was in their faces so their scent, probably fairly rich after some weeks with limited access to showers, did not reach the sheepdog kennels. Also, just below them (or so it seemed) they could hear a generator

A reconstruction of the Landing Zone at Phillips Cove, Pebble Island.

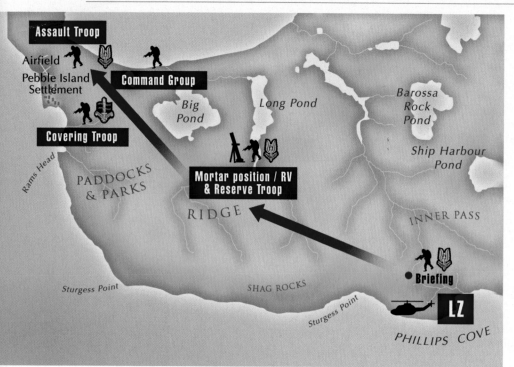

REVISED PLAN AND ROUTES

running, masking all other sounds. Only the day before Second Lieutenant Castro had asked the settlement's mechanic, Norman Morrison, to do a small welding job. It may seem strange that he agreed to help them, but as he said later, it was, *'better than them having a go and ruining the gear.'* Norman had the workshop generator running all day while he was doing the task and in the evening he forgot to switch it from 'RUN' to 'TIMER', so it kept running through the night instead of switching itself off automatically. None of the Argentinians seemed to notice!

At the final rendezvous near the OP, Sergeant Major Gallagher, who was checking-in each Troop as it passed, realised that Mobility Troop had not arrived and immediately advised Major Delves. A quick wireless check revealed that at some point the Troop Commander had lost sight of the man in front. His troop was somewhere down near the ponds – lost. Major Delves called Captain Hamilton, OC Mountain Troop, who, apart from listening into the Squadron net, had just been told by his 'tail-end Charlie' that he was not being followed, although he could not recall exactly when or where the missing men had last been noticed.

There was no time to lose. As the designated reserve for the attack on the airfield, Mountain Troop had not only been as fully briefed as Mobility Troop but had already discussed how they would handle the task. They had, obviously, been issued with plastic explosive, wireless detonators, and wrapping

materials. The main reason why the troop had been designated as the reserve assault force was due to the fact that one of their number, Corporal Raymond Armstrong, a former member of the Royal Green Jackets, was a demolitions expert. He and other members of the troop had made up a number of demolition charges to deal with aircraft and other possible airfield targets.

Led by a delighted Captain Hamilton the Troop took-off for the airfield and were in their forming up position behind the Start Line just before 0700 hrs.

Mobility Troop was the last to leave Phillip's Cove and being at the end of the column and due to shortage of guides were not allocated one. There were only four Boat Troop men, one two-man patrol, which had been near the airfield and only two who had been all the way to the far side of the airfield. Five groups/troops required guides. The other Troops had raced off, crossing the various fences and the wall almost without pause to avoid losing sight of the men in front. There was no tactical crossing of obstacles; if the 'Boss' and Ted Burls hadn't been whacked getting over them then there had obviously been no-one lurking nearby with malice aforethought.

Mobility Troop's OC, however, operated by the book. As the leading man reached an obstacle everyone

> '**The other Troops had raced off, crossing the various fences and the wall almost without pause to avoid losing sight of the men in front.'**

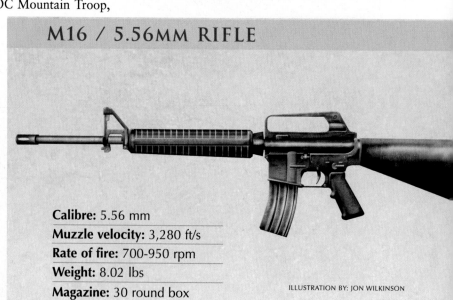

M16 / 5.56MM RIFLE

Calibre:	5.56 mm
Muzzle velocity:	3,280 ft/s
Rate of fire:	700-950 rpm
Weight:	8.02 lbs
Magazine:	30 round box

ILLUSTRATION BY: JON WILKINSON

90

adopted all-round defence. The fence – they never reached the wall – was crossed in accordance with British Army fieldcraft training; weapon made safe, magazine off, on the ground pointing away from the soldier, cross the obstacle, retrieve the weapon, fit the magazine, cock the piece and apply the safety catch, take up a defensive position. As a result, while traversing the undulating terrain of the plateau, Mobility Troop first fell behind then veered off route, went too far down hill and became lost among the broken ground near the wetlands. Worse, someone dropped a weapon near a fence in the bogs by Big Pond. Despite an urgent search it was not found. During that process Major Delves contacted the commanding officer and was told of the situation. As time was running out Mobility were thus allocated the reserve task and told to follow the fence uphill to the crest of the ridge, turn right, and find the mortar site. Quite unmistakable from the flash every time a bomb was fired, despite the weapon being in a dip.

While heading for the airfield Captain Hamilton and Corporal Armstrong had decided to use their limited supply of charges on the Pucaras and any arms and fuel dumps, while their colleagues tackled the Mentors and the Skyvan with small arms, 40mm grenades, and Light Anti-armour Weapons (LAWs). The LAW is a High Explosive Anti-Tank (HEAT) rocket fitted with a shaped-charge warhead. When the rocket strikes the target an instantaneous fuse ignites the charge, turning it into a narrow jet of molten copper alloy. This will penetrate tank armour up to 305mm (12 inches) thick, incinerating the crew, devastating radios

Calibre: 5.56 mm
Muzzle velocity: 3,280 ft/s
Grenade launcher: 40 mm
Weight: 9.8 lbs
Magazine: 30 round box

ILLUSTRATION BY: JON WILKINSON

M16 A1 / M203

and instruments, and detonating unprotected ammunition. LAWs are less effective against aircraft unless fired at fuel tanks, an engine block, or the junction of the main wing spar and the fuselage. Against a twin-engined aircraft such as a Pucara the best effect is likely to be obtained by firing at the nose from dead ahead. That would destroy the instrument panel, and probably detonate the explosive charges in the ejection seats. For single-engined aircraft such as Mentors, the molten jet will destroy the propeller hub, the engine and possibly the control panel. For a Skyvan it can also be used from dead ahead to destroy the control panel or, better still, aimed from the flank at the junction of the shoulder-mounted wing and fuselage to damage or destroy the main spar and rupture and ignite the fuel tanks. Due to the weapon's delayed-arming mechanism it cannot be used less than 10 yards from a target. Even at that range a

The LAW 66 in the process of being fired from a crouched position.

M72 LAW 66

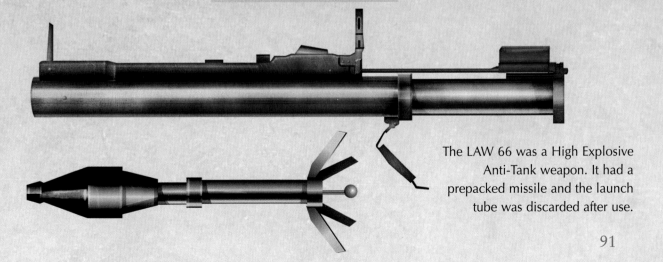

The LAW 66 was a High Explosive Anti-Tank weapon. It had a prepacked missile and the launch tube was discarded after use.

91

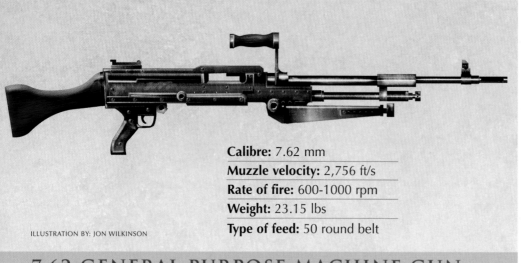

Calibre: 7.62 mm

Muzzle velocity: 2,756 ft/s

Rate of fire: 600-1000 rpm

Weight: 23.15 lbs

Type of feed: 50 round belt

ILLUSTRATION BY: JON WILKINSON

7.62 GENERAL PURPOSE MACHINE GUN

night head-on shot against a small target such as the nose of a small aircraft, seen in the wavering light of parachute flares, would be tricky. There is also the problem of back-blast: highly dangerous for 15 yards behind the firer. The flash will also degrade night-vision for some minutes for anyone within the immediate area unless a warning is yelled by the firer, as is taught in some forces.

At 0700 hrs RALONGS reminded Captain Brown, and through him Major Delves, that *Glamorgan* had to cease fire at 0730. The reply was that that was noted and the airfield assault troop were only now in their forming up positions. The first salvoes were to be Star Shells over target ZJ5007, the approximate area of the Marines' bunkers by the Marble Shanty Track, not high explosive onto target ZJ5004 (the summit of First Mountain, as a diversionary target) as planned. That required *Glamorgan*'s gun crew to change the ammunition loaded into the automatic feed mechanism, which was carried out quickly. The scene was now set for the raid.

Captain Brown called for Star Shell at 0719 hrs. It

was delivered at 0722 hrs and continued with rounds fired at 15 second intervals until high explosive was called for. The first flares immediately revealed the number of aircraft to be attacked (eleven) and their disposition around the airfield – requiring some hasty re-thinking on the part of Captain Hamilton and his men.

It also produced what Captain Brown later described as, *'an immediate response from the enemy, who were obviously forewarned, and were in the hills above Pebble Island Settlement'*. There is no note of any such response in the Argentinian Separata No 20; but it is reasonable to assume that a spooked sentry may have fired in reaction to the flare.

In reply to the enemy intervention Major Delves, through Captain Brown, called for high explosive and via the SAS net, for Para-Illumination rounds from the mortar. The high explosive was delivered onto target ZJ5007, with, as has been noted above, commendable accuracy, given that there had been no ranging shots. Target ZJ5007 was the col on the eastern flank of First Mountain, which dominated the airfield area and was the obvious place for defences such as GPMG – operating in the sustained fire role – mortar and recoilless rifle pits. According to Captain Brown, the whole of the ridge was neutralised by spreading fire, with the rounds being 'walked' downhill towards the settlement. It was checked just as Mountain Troop reached the edge of the airfield without having come under enemy fire-effective or otherwise; the few Marines on the airfield having been effectively suppressed.

Whilst Corporal Armstrong and Captain Hamilton

First Mountain looming over the airfield. ALLAN WHITE

tackled the Pucaras, their colleagues raced to their designated targets and set about them with M16/M203s, GPMGs and LAWs. Everyone realised they were perpetuating the work of such SAS legends as Bob Bennett, Johnny Cooper, Dave Kershaw and above all, Paddy Main; destroyers of aircraft par excellence, despite having different weapons.

DISABLING AIRCRAFT

In 1941, at RAF Heliopolis, L Detachment SAS Brigade learned how to sabotage aircraft and airfield equipment to maximum effect. Jock Lewes, David Stirling, Bill Cumper and other 'Originals' were taught by a Scottish RAFVR engineering officer and his long-serving (and long-suffering) Flight Sergeant.

Between 1945 and the Pebble Island Raid in 1982, British SAS troops, as far as can be discerned from open sources, did not attack aircraft or airfields but the basic techniques did not change over the years. If aircraft cannot be destroyed outright a number of the same type can be immobilised by demolishing a common item on each, making cannibalisation difficult or impossible, depending on the spares situation on the airfield. Hence the need for observers and CTR teams to locate the engineering workshop and stores on a target airfield. Nose-wheel tyres or instrument panels can be shattered by small arms fire. Landing-gear leg hinges can be destroyed with small demolition charges or damaged by grenades thus collapsing the aircraft and probably causing structural damage. Improvised airfields such as Pebble Island are rarely supplied with a mobile crane, making recovery and repair of 'dropped' aircraft almost impossible.

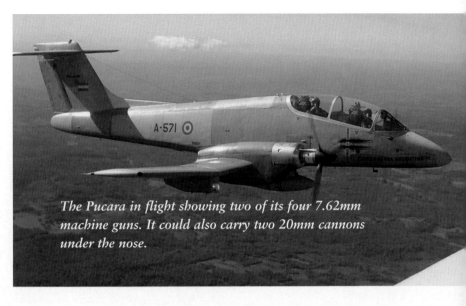

The Pucara in flight showing two of its four 7.62mm machine guns. It could also carry two 20mm cannons under the nose.

Corporal Armstrong worked his way round the aircraft, distributing his charges with care. The Pucaras, including the ditched A-523, had charges placed inside the undercarriage wells of the engine nacelles, or were strapped to undercarriage leg-joints with adhesive tape.

The four Mentors, A-401, A-408, A-411 and A-412 each received two charges, one under the port tail-plane, the other under the engine, inside the nose-wheel bay. Aviation fuel and ammunition 'dumps' could not be located. Several drums of JP-1 were found, some by accident, when they were hit by small-arms fire. That included those in the small *depositivo combustivo* by the Fire Tender Hut.

Lieutenant Marega had placed a small night guard of six Marines on the airfield – two in the fire tender hut and four in a roamer patrol. When the first flares ignited the guards in the hut telephoned Lieutenant Marega, who had heard *Glamorgan*'s gunfire, he had already

AI-58 PUCARA

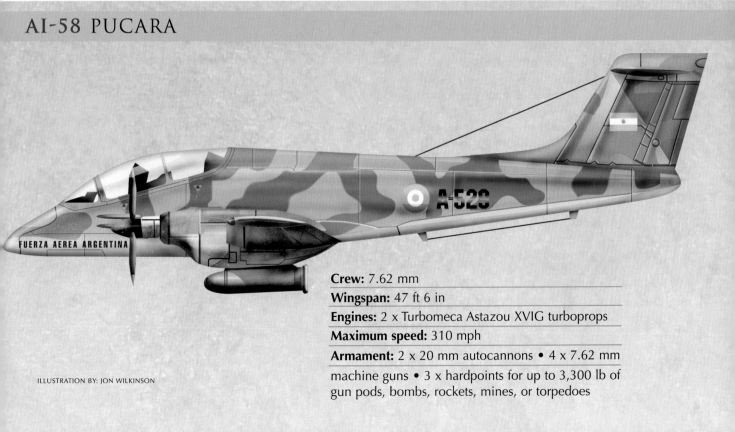

ILLUSTRATION BY: JON WILKINSON

Crew: 7.62 mm	
Wingspan: 47 ft 6 in	
Engines: 2 x Turbomeca Astazou XVIG turboprops	
Maximum speed: 310 mph	
Armament: 2 x 20 mm autocannons • 4 x 7.62 mm machine guns • 3 x hardpoints for up to 3,300 lb of gun pods, bombs, rockets, mines, or torpedoes	

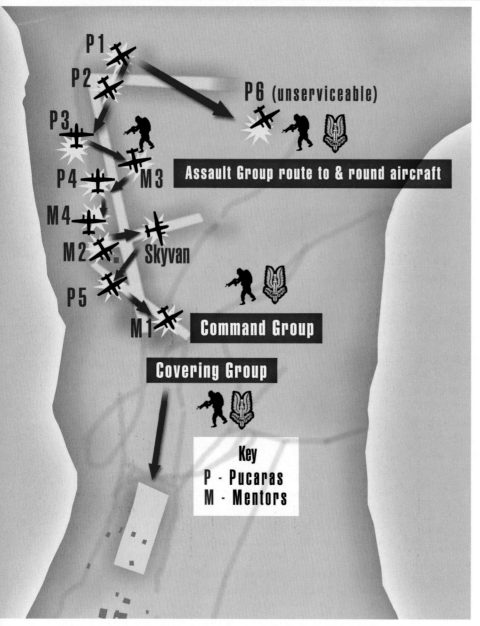

P1
P2
P6 (unserviceable)
P3

Assault Group route to & round aircraft

P4 M3
M4
M2 Skyvan
P5
M1 Command Group

Covering Group

Key
P - Pucaras
M - Mentors

THE PROGRESSION OF THE ATTACK

realised the expected attack had started. The other officers in the School/Mess were also awake and Lieutenant Castro telephoned a contact report to the CCM in Stanley.

Argentinian accounts differ from the time the British high explosive shells started to thump First Mountain but it appears as though Lieutenant Marega, a Marine NCO and an engineer Corporal headed first for the DFCC to test the firing circuit and then attach the detonating wires and cord to the detonator and igniter. The Corporal remained in the centre while the two Marines, weapons in hand, crept up the slope leading to the airfield and peered over the edge. Due to the terrain they had to stand to see anything and witnessed a number of shadowy figures running towards and around the parked aircraft, pausing only to fire weapons or throw hand grenades.

The two Marines made their way towards the fire tender hut. They were spotted and challenged by the two guards, and went inside. Everyone crouched on the floor

as there were small arms rounds cracking past the hut at odd intervals. The guards reported that they were huddled in the hut, more or less out of the wind, when they were galvanised by the distant blast of Glamorgan's first rounds. Each shot briefly lit up the night sky to the northeast. Those first rounds were followed by a barrage of star-shell and then mortar, flares and HE shells bursting apparently above the guards on First Mountain. These explosions were succeeded by streams of GPMG tracer rounds going into and through aircraft, small arms fire, grenade and LAW blasts. The SAS mortar flare illumination was intermittent. Every two or three rounds the mortar base-plate sank into the soft soil of the dell and had to be hauled out, re-positioned and the barrel re-aligned.

One of the 40mm grenades caused an own goal; Corporal Davey, Mountain Troop, was hit in the leg by a splinter. He was immediately attended to by his patrol commander, Staff Sergeant Philip Currass, D Squadron's Royal Army Medical Corps specialist. (Currass was also a fully-trained SAS operator, boat-handler, troop 2i/c and patrol leader.) Corporal Davey was more annoyed than hurt and after treatment was able to hobble back to the rendezvous, where he was again examined, given further attention to his leg and sent back to the mortar pit with an escort-cum-guide; both men disappointed at missing the action.

A further spectacular effect occurred when something – 7.62mm GPMG, 5.56mm M16 rounds or grenade splinter – breached the fuel tank of Lieutenant Pereya's Mentor A-401, aircraft, releasing fuel onto the grass. Another something, perhaps a tracer round, parachute flare, LAW rocket or 40mm grenade fragment, ignited the petrol soaking into the grass strip. The fuel around the aircraft erupted in flames. The Argentinian roamer patrol was spotted near the Guard Hut, where Lieutenant Marega was trying to figure out what was happening. He ordered the patrol to take some chemical fire extinguishers, standard equipment for a light aircraft base, and tackle the blaze. When some of the raiders saw the figures emerge from the hut carrying the bulky objects they opened fire on them. The marines dropped their loads, took cover as best they could by the hut and returned fire at shadowy, half glimpsed figures racing around the airfield. The SAS raiders returned fire but for only a brief period, as the Marines' shooting was not effective. The defensive fire seems to have continued for some time, possibly until the Marines ran out of ammunition or their ardour was suppressed by accurate

ILLUSTRATION BY: JON WILKINSON

PNA SKYVAN PA-50

return fire. Several accounts state that as the raiders withdrew, two Argentinians, presumably Lieutenant Marega, and an NCO, attempted to intervene. They reportedly yelled at their men to rally and open fire and opened fire themselves in the general direction of the vague shapes seen amongst the smoke from the explosions, fires, flares and by the light of the intermittent moonlight. Their efforts were silenced by a blizzard of small-arms fire and M-203 grenades. Roger Edwards recalled that,

'there was a very short firefight on the strip and a couple of Argentinians were slightly wounded, I do not remember anyone being killed.'

The SAS barrier group did not open fire although they were ready to do so if any Argentinians attempted to advance up the slope in front of them leading to the airstrips. None did. Discretion was the better part of valour that night and in any case the only 'tooth-arm' officer, Lieutenant Marega, was on the airfield.

The last shot, so to speak, fired by defenders caused the gravest injury suffered by the SAS. Just as Corporal Armstrong was trying to attach a charge to the sixth Pucara, A-523, down by the eastern end of the northerly airstrip, Lieutenant Marega ordered the detonation of the airfield demolition charges. Corporal Armstrong was blown off his feet, severely shaken, and was deafened for some days afterwards but was otherwise unhurt.

Lieutenant Marega had assessed that the British might be about to land Hercules transports carrying a follow-up force onto the airfield and intended to deny them use of the main airstrip. The result was a considerable tribute to the skill of the combat engineers. All of

the charges went off, blowing neat, deep craters. Unfortunately the Skyvan aircraft was parked over the middle of a line of charges and destroyed.

The demolition charges also caused another minor casualty. According to Roger Edwards,

'when the demolition team were withdrawing from the strip a command-detonated mine was set off slightly injuring two of the boys (ears rang for a week I was told).'

Corporal Bunker, Mountain Troop, was blown over and concussed by the blast; he had already been injured in the Wessex crashes on Fortuna Glacier. He, too, was helped back to the mortar pit, where the reserve troop had helped extricate the weapon and collect any unopened carriers. Uncased rounds were then fired-off and the empty cases left behind, trophies for the garrison, later to be requisitioned by security personnel.

Time was getting short; sunrise would be at 0728 hrs

An aerial photograph showing craters in the airstrip blown by the Argentine Marine Engineers during the attack.

Pucara A-529. IAN HOWAT

Mentor 412. IAN HOWAT

Mentor 408. IAN HOWAT

Above: A close shot of a Pucara showing damage caused by small arms fire. Below: Another wrecked Pucara with triple ejection racks showing under the outer wings. IAN HOWAT

but there would be light before that to assist a determined attack by Pucaras from Stanley or Condor on Pebble Island, or by an Exocet-armed aircraft from the Argentinian mainland. Therefore the pick-up, return flight and departure of the Carrier Group had to be completed as soon as possible. On Captain Hamilton's signal the demolition charges were blown and more small arms, GPMG and LAW fire opened on aircraft lacking demolition charges. The results, coupled with the wavering light from the star shells and mortar bombs, were spectacular. A signal was sent to *Hermes* stating the attack had been successful and requesting evacuation. The carrier and *Broadsword* were moving towards the helicopter recovery position. That decision had been taken some time before following urgent discussions between various naval command and staff officers, Tactical HQ and Major Delves, since the delays, coupled with distance, the weather and the approach of sunrise indicated an early departure.

AIRCRAFT DESTROYED
TEN OR ELEVEN?

Most English language accounts of the raid state that eleven aircraft were destroyed. However, all Argentinian sources, including the official FAA website and those of other Argentinian armed forces and the PNA, admit to only ten; five Pucaras, four Mentors and a Skyvan. To quote, *'en seta operation, la FAA perdió los* IA-58 Pucará matrículas A-502, A-520, A-526, A-529, A-552.

The discrepancy is to due to Pucara A-523 having been struck-off the strength following its hard landing. The SAS attacked it, however, unaware of its state, and it was seriously damaged.

Lit by the glare of flares and a burning aircraft the raiders withdrew. The garrison did not appear to have any plan for dealing with a raid, although someone managed to transmit a message which eventually found its way to the command centre in Stanley. There was not much that could be done to help due to the lack of night-flying equipment at the air bases and in the helicopters, Pucaras and Mentors and even less experience of night anti-helicopter operations by any of the aircrew. The clumsy chain of command at Borbon; naval aviation, marines, air force and coastguard, hardly helped matters. There was no lack of courage, but also no experience of being under fire and no tradition of airfield defence as taught by the RAF Regiment and practised by all ranks on British military airfields during Tactical Evaluation exercises.

When the entire raiding party had been checked through the rendezvous and assembled close to the mortar pit, they took off eastwards; exhaustion overcome by the adrenalin 'high' of a close quarters contact. The raiders travelled in a fast moving column of Troops, with an advance guard to deal with an ambush and a rear guard trotting behind in case of pursuit. Under Captain Brown's control, *Glamorgan* laid down a curtain of fire onto First Mountain which was gradually 'walked' westwards along the north flank as if covering

An aerial photograph showing the extent of the damage the morning after the raid.

a withdrawal towards the area around Marble Shanty.

The Sea Kings were on their way, flying in from the Ship Harbour area to meet the withdrawing troops. This was a considerable risk. No-one could be sure the garrison did not have 81 or 120mm mortars, an ideal method of illuminating then harassing withdrawing troops and deadly against a helicopter landing zone, especially one being used for a 'hot extraction'.

The Sea Kings spotted and headed towards the marshaller's torches. A rolling rendezvous was achieved about two miles from the airfield; a last-minute barrage from *Glamorgan* was laid down between the SAS party and the settlement. It ceased at 0745 hrs, once the helicopters signalled that the raiding party had embarked. *Glamorgan* then departed with all speed.

The raiding force boarded the helicopters and returned to *Hermes*, which was loitering, bows down wind, ready to turn about and depart at high speed once the Sea Kings were secured on deck.

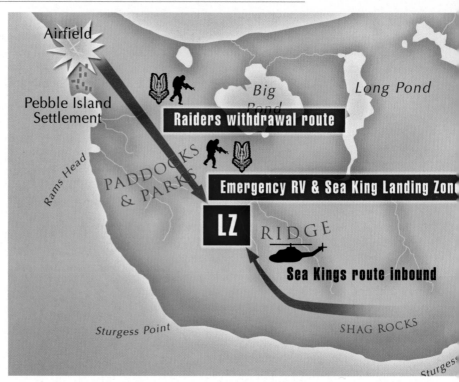

ROUTE OF WITHDRAWAL AND LIFT-OFF

A relieved Roger Edwards later recalled that,

'we got back to Hermes *in time for breakfast and she was soon speeding east just as fast as she could go.'*

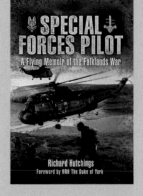